CW00829110

10/03/03

Happy Birthday Christopher.
May you be happy &
successful in all you do.

Love,
        Dad & Mum.
                xxxx

WAYNE BENNETT

WAYNE BENNETT

DON'T DIE WITH THE MUSIC IN YOU

WITH STEVE CRAWLEY

ABC
BOOKS

Published by ABC Books for the
AUSTRALIAN BROADCASTING CORPORATION
GPO Box 9994 Sydney NSW 2001

Copyright © Wayne Bennett and Crawley & Associates 2002

First published May 2002
Reprinted May 2002 (twice)
Reprinted June 2002 (twice)
Reprinted July 2002

All rights reserved. No part of this publication may be reproduced,
stored in a retrieval system or transmitted in any form or by any means,
electronic, mechanical, photocopying, recording or otherwise, without
the prior written permission of the Australian Broadcasting Corporation.

National Library of Australia
Cataloguing-in-Publication entry
Bennett, Wayne, 1950– .
   Don't die with the music in you.

   ISBN 0 7333 1107 5.
   1. Bennett, Wayne, 1950– . 2. Brisbane Broncos (Football team)
   – History. 3. Football coaches – Australia – Biography.
   4. Rugby League Football – Australia – History.
   I. Australian Broadcasting Corporation. II. Title.

796.3338092

Produced by Geoff Armstrong
Cover designed by Nine Hundred VC
Internal design and layout by Graeme Jones, Kirby/Jones Design
Set in 10.5/15 Giovanni Book
Colour reproduction by Colorwize Studio, Adelaide
Printed and bound in Australia by Griffin Press, Adelaide

54.5 - 8 7 6

"My life has been adversity, but from each disaster I've come back stronger. I don't fear what's happening, I know how to battle through it. I know I'll come out the other side of it and I know they'll come out with me. It's just a matter of when and we'll be better for it. We'll be stronger people. We'll appreciate winning more than we ever have in the past . . ."

— **Wayne Bennett** (from the *Australian Story* episode "Man For All Seasons", quoted after the Brisbane Broncos had lost seven and drawn one of their first nine games in 1999)

CONTENTS

INTRODUCTION

By STEVE CRAWLEY

WAYNE BENNETT IS A CONTRADICTION. HAD THOMAS EDISON PUT enough time aside to work him out, we'd still be sitting in the dark. For all the gnarl, he's a recent Queensland Father of the Year, and when the ABC's *Australian Story* showcased him and his family it achieved record ratings and remarkable responses to the softness of it all. He's on the speaking circuit yet the football media rarely gets a go with him. Publicly, he's Clint Eastwood without the Magnum. Privately, though, in the confines of his football teams, he is not just respected but revered.

His players play for *him*, and he trains them for *them*, unequivocally. It's almost perfect — the Brisbane Broncos having won all five grand finals they have contested (1992, 1993, 1997, 1998, 2000), and Queensland, in five years of his coaching, having lost just one series, 1986 (with wins in 1987, 1988, 1998 and 2001). Before he became the Broncos' inaugural coach in 1988, he was the co-coach of the Canberra Raiders when that club reached the NSW Rugby League grand final for the first time, having coached Brothers and Souths with success in the Brisbane premiership during the early 1980s.

"You have a choice in life," Bennett explained during the 2001 State of Origin series, "you can sit back and criticise or you can try to make a difference."

At the time, I was developing a profile of the coach for *The Sydney Morning Herald*. I have to admit that, despite Wayne's often stressed relationship with the media, this wasn't the toughest assignment of my journalistic career. I have been the "with" bit of Wayne Bennett's newspaper columns on football and life since 1993. Indeed, some of the material in this book has been adapted from those columns, while other parts are new, written especially for here.

In the process, I've got to know the bloke a little. I know he is pig-headed, and gnarly. I think he at times sets out to intimidate people. And don't worry about him being misunderstood, because that's the way he plans it. But if I was in the trenches, I'd want him beside me. Say Mars was coming our way to war, and I had to pick one earthling to go out and plot our defence, to fight to the end, that earthling would be Wayne James Bennett.

At 53, he's still fit enough, aerobically, to play the game in which he represented Queensland (1971–73) and Australia on the 1971 tour of New Zealand. For a morning training session with the Queensland team the squad was split into three groups. One completed two seven-minute runs back-to-back, before another performed the same gut-buster. Bennett ran with all three groups and did not finish further back than fourth.

"I just love running with them," he said. "You do feel a lot closer to them when you're out there putting in together, and you're all hurting together, pushing each other and that. I wish I could play with them ..."

Apart from raw ability, the first thing Bennett looks for in an athlete is commitment. He looks at his team and sees a lot of guys with varying personalities but with a common attribute — commitment. The second thing is trust. He's got to be able to trust them. That's what he looks for in all of his relationships. "I'll forgive a young player if he tells me a lie," he says, "but I won't forgive him twice."

Some of the finest men he's met have been footballers. They've had a big influence on him, he says, on who he is and what he is. His uncle Eddie Brosnan. Basil Phelan, a Darling Downs farmer. Men such as Jack Gibson and Ron Massey, Don Furner and Bob Bax. Coaches, administrators. Paul Morgan was another guy; an ex-footballer too, Porky.

"Look at Big Gordie [Gorden Tallis, the current Broncos and Queensland captain]," he said after that training session in 2001. "He has values, and he won't negotiate with anybody. If I've got a problem with Gorden, I ring his Mum and say, 'Handle him, Jude.' He's just got a determination about him, a complete honesty. He gets that steely look in his eyes, which he does every so often, and he says: 'Coach, you just tell me what I have to do — and I'll do it.'" The respect and admiration Bennett has for his captain shines through.

During training, Bennett said many things, some non-negotiable: "No shortcuts," he said often. "Discipline." "Help each other out." "Good work." "We're in it together, guys." "Good stuff." "Do something you don't want to do . . . this is when you're tired."

But the five words barked with greatest emphasis were: "Don't stop three steps short." This had to do with the seven-minute runs, when one of the forwards slowed down just short of the finish line, a concrete slab.

"It's a state of mind," says Bennett. "Three steps won't make any difference fitness-wise but three steps make all the difference to the psyche. You know you haven't taken a shortcut, you know when you're tired you've found something. And that's what they're going to be on Sunday. When they get to that point they know they can go those extra three steps because they have to.

"The kind of people who stop three steps short, I wouldn't call them losers but they're never winners either. They always fall short. They're in all forms of life. Great ability, talent . . . they just won't make those three last steps."

Steve Crawley is recognised as one of Australia's leading sports writers, having won several major awards for his writing on rugby league, horse racing and tennis. He has held senior columnist positions with *The Sun*, *The Sydney Morning Herald*, *The Herald-Sun* and *The Australian*, and served as turf editor of *The Telegraph-Mirror* and sports editor of *The Sun-Herald*. He was the founding executive producer of Channel 10's *Sports Tonight*, and for the past seven years has found a home at Network Seven, in varying roles from Sports Editor to General Manager, Sport.

FOREWORDS

By VANESSA GORMAN
(Producer, *Australian Story*)

WHEN I WAS FIRST ASKED TO PRODUCE AN *AUSTRALIAN STORY* for ABC Television about Wayne Bennett, I am embarrassed to admit my first words were, "Who's Wayne Bennett?"

I knew next to nothing about the inner workings of rugby league and felt inadequate to tackle someone I quickly discovered was a legend. Even scarier was his reputation with the press. But as Wayne said, "If telling my story helps only one other person then it's probably worth doing."

Wayne trusted our program's reputation enough to open up to us completely. He shared the hardships of his childhood and early life, and his family allowed our cameras into their home to witness the daily struggles of caring for two disabled children.

Wayne and his serene and beautiful wife Trish had faced the heartbreak of seeing their firstborn son Justin become mentally disabled after an adverse reaction to immunisation needles. Elizabeth was their first daughter and then Katherine was born with physical disabilities that have left her wheelchair-bound.

The courage and acceptance they displayed left me profoundly moved. More than that, I feel privileged to have witnessed the joy and love that is also part of their daily family life.

I came to see the other side of the stony-faced Bennett portrayed in the media. The loving and gentle father and the mentor of many hundreds of young footballers he has coached over the years. The strong role model who made a promise to his mother not to smoke or drink or gamble like his father, and who has made something extraordinary of his life despite the odds being stacked against him.

Wayne's public successes in football speak for themselves. But it was the private man I came to admire, a man who has touched and inspired a wider audience. From "Who's Wayne Bennett?", I can now honestly state that I count him as one of my heroes.

By LACHLAN MURDOCH
(Deputy Chief Operating Officer, News Corporation)

FOOTBALL IS A GAME FOR HARD MEN AND NO ONE HAS PLAYED IT harder than Wayne Bennett. Year after year he has been in the spotlight bringing some of us the joy of victory and others the dismay of defeat. Yet he has resolutely remained the quiet man of rugby league.

Wayne Bennett's chosen career means his wins and losses are very public, but he loathes the limelight. While he's been in the public eye for decades we have known very little about him.

To many, the ABC's *Australian Story* on the Bennett family was a revelation. Wayne was revealed as an unexpectedly gentle man whose gentleness was forged by personal hardship and challenge.

We now know he's a man whose success is built on loyalty, discipline and an innate recognition of individual worth. He is a collector of quotes and a source of wisdom to many.

Now Wayne's not perfect. One day I hope he will revise his poor opinion of the media.

His decision to write this book, however, offers everyone the chance to understand how he's made his life such a success, and made the Broncos and the Maroons forces to be reckoned with.

By GED NOLAN
(Ged The Farmer)

OUR ASSOCIATION WITH WAYNE, TRISH, JUSTIN, BETH AND KATH started several years ago, through Bas and Betty Phelan of Berat near Allora on Queensland's Darling Downs.

Wayne has a special part in his heart for these two people, as he spent some of his childhood on the Phelans farm. Wayne has often quoted the great practical advice given to him as a small boy, then later to him as a parent, said so clearly it didn't fall on deaf ears.

As we lived close by, Bet thought it would be great for Justin to watch a few cows being milked. Since then Justin and Wayne have been regulars.

When Wayne and Justin come to visit us on the farm it doesn't matter to us that he is the Broncos coach. His football credentials go out the door when he becomes a man on the land.

Things have to be done on the farm and there is always a right and wrong way of doing them. Even though at times Wayne has mucked up, he is always willing to listen and learn. Occasionally, though, the wax would have been blown clean out of his ears due to copping a blast from a frustrated farmer.

There have been many discussions in the kitchen and up at the dairy on matters some people are hesitant to discuss with Wayne — matters he needs to hear.

Wayne finds refuge in the farming atmosphere away from the city lights, demanding pressures and interfering media. It's here, while he is washing out the dairy or chipping burrs, that the tall, quiet man of strong, steady leadership thinks — maybe of what he is going to say to some less-fortunate boys, to a group of multi corporate executives or to his players. Or how he is going to persuade Justin to get into the car to go home from the farm.

We have come to know the other side of Wayne Bennett — his generosity, a trait he has inherited from his mum, Patsy, and the way he treats everyone with respect and as equals.

Wayne has a gift of listening to others and this is shown in the way the players confide in him. On the farm, we often say Wayne treats his players the same way he treats his cows — he never wants to sell or retire them.

Wayne has an exceptional character, and a dry wit, and is an example to young people to avoid gambling and drinking in excess.

To be able to count a man of this calibre as our family friend is a real blessing.

By STEVE WAUGH

(Australian Test Cricket Captain)

For me, Wayne Bennett's greatest strength is the simplicity of his message. What he says is commonsense. Further to that, he treats sportspeople as human beings first, sportspeople second. I admire his people management skills; that he is able to treat different people differently, according to how he sees them. In doing so, he gets the most from his players and his team.

You can't help but be impressed by the man and his record. I put great value in the fact that I know that what he says actually works. This is not some young bloke spouting forth the latest theory or some new fad. With Wayne, you know he's been through some tough times, that his every word reflects his vast experience and the many successes his teams have enjoyed.

Knowing how much stress and pressure there is in modern professional team sports, I find it amazing that he's stayed motivated for so long. But he loves his job, the game, being around and helping the guys, loves dealing with the many different characters who make up the sport. The ongoing challenge clearly stimulates him. Most importantly, he does what he does for the team, not for the publicity or the accolades that might come his way. Personal triumphs don't interest him; rather, he wants to achieve success as one part of a group.

Wayne is pretty good mates with John Buchanan, the coach of the Australian cricket team, while for me, he's become something of a "long-distance" mentor, someone I can learn a great deal from through observing him at work and sharing the occasional conversation. "Buck" and I invited Wayne to come and talk to the Australian one-day side after we lost three consecutive games at the start of 2002, and his message had an immediate impact. Looking back, he didn't say much, but what he said was right on the money. He reminded us that we had achieved plenty in the previous couple of years, and suggested that nothing had changed except, most likely, our attitudes. If we went back to basics everything would be OK. Again, simple, commonsense stuff. He kept things in terms we could relate to and gave us advice we could put into action. We won four of our next five games.

This wasn't the first time Wayne had talked to the Australian team. Every time it's the same. He doesn't overstate things, comes in, says what needs to be said —

it might take 10, 15 or 20 minutes, never too long — and gets his points across very easily.

From time to time, people ask me what "mental toughness" is. I've heard Wayne Bennett define it as the ability not to give in to yourself. To me, that's exactly what being mentally tough is — not taking the easy option, keeping your concentration focused no matter what's happening around you. If you have a plan and a goal, you've got to stick by it. If you're in a difficult situation or things are going against you, you've got to believe in yourself and what you want to do.

The easy option, of course, is to say that it's all too hard, to try something different. Trust me, if you want to be mentally tough, do as Wayne Bennett says: follow your beliefs and don't give in to yourself.

COACHING

"Thinking about ploughing doesn't get the job done ..."

SO, YOU WANT TO BE A COACH?

MAYBE JACK GIBSON DIDN'T INVENT THE SAYING, BUT SOMEHOW he made it his own. "If it ain't broke," the master coach would say, "don't fix it." Then another coach said, "If it ain't broke — then break it." Both have merit, but are not always easy to do.

Many people say many things about coaching, like: "We're going to have a good year if our coaching staff lives up to its potential." And, "Coaching is like being a King — it prepares you for nothing." In America, if you're a coach in the NFL it means: Not For Long.

One guy says, "If I win a big game I like my players to be strong enough to carry me off the field", while his players huddle in corners whispering, "When we come out of the tunnel we always try not to stand next to the coach because the fans throw beer at him."

People coach for a couple of reasons. One's ego, while for others it represents continued involvement in the game they love. I coach because I like being part of a team, and I can't play any more. It's not something I planned to do. I was working as a policeman at Petrie, playing first-grade football with a bit of a profile when I stumbled on a team that needed a coach — Under 20s in the Church League.

Oh, there's another reason people coach: because they think they can.

The most important thing a coach needs is the ability to communicate. Sure, knowledge of the game is high on the list of requirements, but communication is an absolute must. Communication is not always about talking. In fact, you can talk too much. Listening is the art of communication. It's not what you say, it's what they hear.

Also, a coach needs a vision, for want of a better word. Going into a club, you have to know what type of football you're going to play, how you're going to achieve it and be realistic about what you have to achieve it with.

Over the years you build and develop that vision.

Besides communication, the trick is getting people to work together, and you've got to be prepared to lead.

One aspect you can't lack is confidence because many times things won't be working out and the stands will be full enough with doubting people without you jumping up and joining them. And there are times when you doubt yourself, but they can't be long times.

It's true, I now cringe at the memory of some of my early coaching performances. But I didn't cringe then. I thought I was OK.

Bob Bax rates among the great coaches Queensland has produced, taking his ability as a good communicator and adding motivation and inspiration. He did things way before his time.

Jack Gibson was different to Bax in that he said so few words but they made so much sense. He was just right. I never played under Jack, but you always felt that he cared. More about him later.

A player has to know the coach cares about him. Bax cared, too, and we cared about him in return.

The fact is, most coaches have different coaching styles and it is difficult to say what makes one successful and the other a flop. In truth, you can do too much for players because you don't want them dying in your arms. And if you don't give them responsibility, that's what they'll do. Just up and die.

No doubt some players are easier to coach than others, the ones who'll do anything, who'll sacrifice, for the team. Even they have egos, but they can leave them at the dressing-room door and there's no price they wouldn't pay for the team.

Individual sacrifice punctuates every session and play, because never will 13 guys agree at the very same time, which makes for a real juggling act.

So what's most important: a good coach or a good captain? I'd have to say a good captain.

A good coach with a bad captain? He's struggling.

A good captain with a bad coach? He's making the coach look good.

What makes one club successful and another spending the same money and putting in the same hours unsuccessful is, first up, the chairman or chief executive or a combination of both. Strong people in the front office attract other strong people, whether it be in sport or business — not that there is any difference these days.

Bob Bax, whenever reflecting on being young and just kicking off coaching in the bush, would say how he'd seek out the most influential person in the team and make him his best mate and captain. How it worked every time.

The rewards are again different with different people. Most coaches would rather be a player, because the real rewards are playing with the guys. Out there, you can make things happen. Up in the stands, after you've bought an ice cream, a program and consulted the referee from some distance about his parentage, there's not a whole lot you can make happen.

Fans overrate the role of a coach. This I know, because I just can't believe any coach is as good as they think they are, nor as bad.

An Aussie rules player in South Australia made for interesting reading when he finished second last on the table one year, switched clubs, and won the comp the next. Surrounded afterwards by reporters, he said the coach at the bottom club was superior to the coach at the premier club, which is something I can comprehend.

When things aren't going well, I think it's bloody stupid to blame the coach.

I will say, though, that no matter what sport you coach at the top level — do an apprenticeship. Do your time. Make your mistakes somewhere else.

Coaching today is much more than tactics and tackling, with complexities reaching far beyond kick-off and fulltime. In the long run, though, it's true: coaching does prepare you for nothing.

And before you go, there is one more statement from a coach I like: "A team should be an extension of a coach's personality." My teams are always smiling and yapping to the media.

THE FUN CAN WAIT UNTIL AFTER THE GAME

Rightly or wrongly, I have a pretty dour image when it comes to sitting in the stands at rugby league matches, and, it's true, I do see it as my office.

Everything I have done all week rides on Sunday, the only day of the week I have so little control over, yet with everything depending on it.

The difficult thing about coaching is that the players can — and you can — do a great job all week only to see it fall to bits on Sunday.

I remember Jack Gibson saying Sunday was his day off, but could never quite work out that one. I've been there, to the wall, a lot of times but still on many days I'm nervous, shadow boxing butterflies.

Often, I can't see what the opposition's doing, and after a game when someone says so-and-so had a great match for them, I just hunch my shoulders, say, "Right."

To me, the enjoyment is after the game. Those five minutes, that half an hour. Maybe even the whole night. That is something you cannot replace.

There are two questions I get most asked, the first one being: "Are you going to win today?" As if I know. It fascinates me how punters go up to horse trainers, asking: "How's Radish going to aim up today?" All the trainer knows is that Radish has trained well, he hasn't a clue how Licorice from the other stable is feeling.

The second most asked question is: "What did you say to them at halftime?" To be honest, I have two speeches: one for when we're winning, it's in the right pocket; and one for when we're losing — it's in the left.

DOING THE HARD THING

IN 1995, WE LOST A MATCH AGAINST ILLAWARRA. IT REMAINS one of the most disappointing performances in the club's history, but there was no indication it was coming before the match.

I have my own way of handling such disappointments: going into a cave where I say nothing, knowing words mean so little. After a loss I don't normally go on but I did this time, telling the players of my disappointment in them, that there was no way they could possibly look one another in the eye and say they'd done their best. I looked up and 15 heads were down.

My wife, being perceptive, watches me get around the house head down in such weeks, mumbling, looking for the dog I don't own to kick. She says: "I couldn't do the job you do."

After that Illawarra game, I had a week thinking about the job I do, in more detail than ever before. My initial feeling was I just don't want to do it any more. I don't want to go through this. Knowing my mood swings and feelings, that was quite normal.

My other tendency is to begin soul searching: Did I do a good enough job? Was it my fault entirely?

The only redeeming thing about Sundays like that one is the night's sleep. I hardly ever watch television but this time I sat right through *Joseph*, a biblical story with some good messages. I wasn't looking for messages, just tiredness for a good night's sleep. It worked.

I woke up a lot more positive, still not feeling good, but positive about what had to be done.

One thing I've learned in life is perseverance. Most importantly, you need to know where you're going, but secondly, you have to persevere.

So often we are so close to our objectives, only to walk away. Pioneers Burke and Wills died of thirst not knowing there was water over the very next hill.

At the time we think the hard thing is to walk away. We assure ourselves of that, but it's not. The hard thing is to stay, to persevere.

By Monday, I was in perseverance mode.

Facing the videos on Monday is extremely difficult, knowing you're not going to see anything that hasn't beaten you before.

Then to team selections.

The previous year when we'd struggled, I persevered too long with players because of reputations. That was perceived as a weakness, but we'd been through so much together. With some players it had been eight years, through all the highs and lows, and if there was any doubt I wanted to give them the benefit of my loyalty.

You can adopt that scorched-earth policy and burn everyone and everything in front of you, but that's quick-fix stuff, not a long-term remedy.

You have relationships but I promised myself during the off-season that if we ever went through this again I wouldn't be weak, I wouldn't make speeches — just take firm action.

If someone was a lair, or didn't train well or had a bad attitude, it would be easy to drop him. But the people who make up the Broncos have no such traits, they're good people. They don't go out to fail, and are guilty at times only of not preparing well enough for a match.

Monday afternoon's team meeting was not a pleasant experience, telling the players involved they wouldn't be in the first-grade squad . . . no joy at all.

From fulltime on Sunday we lived in our own little hell, but by Tuesday morning I'm starting to come out of the cave.

I realise it's important for me to be positive for the team. By positive I don't mean going around kidding ourselves, but at least looking forward to the next game. When I left that team meeting I said I didn't want to hear another word about Illawarra.

If you keep looking over your shoulder, it won't be long before you are going backwards.

My farmer friend Ged rang through the week, sounding more disappointed than me, and said just one thing: "Thinking about the ploughing doesn't get it done."

Losing is not the issue here, never has been. I've been around this game long enough to understand there has to be a loser, but no matter how long I'm around I'll never tolerate guys not giving their best.

What fascinates me is that people can take a knock at work and everyone understands when they have trouble finding the motivation to go back to the office. Everyone thinks footballers are different.

They're wrong.

TALENT IS ONLY THE BEGINNING

THE CURIOUSLY NAMED FORMER NFL COACH, BUM PHILLIPS, warned that everyone forgets you once you leave the game. "And all you will have left," said Bum, "are the things it has taught you: to sacrifice, to work hard, to never give in . . . you'll be able to use these things for the rest of your life."

Today, I look at the emerging stars of our game and what I see is great talent. Talent, though, is only the beginning.

In the book, *Why We Win*, the UCLA basketball coach from 1964 to 1975, John Wooden, got me thinking when he said he sometimes heard other coaches saying, "He's potentially the best player I've had." Wooden tells them, "You explain yourself when you say 'potentially'."

You're not saying he is the best player — you're saying "potentially". They don't pay off on potential. They pay off on results — how you produce. So if he's just potential, he's not your best player. Someone else who doesn't have that potential might be your best player.

Although this other player is a lesser talent, it might be better for other players to be on the floor or out on the field with him than it would be for them to be out there with the big potential guy.

For all the possible future stars there have been a lot of failures and, even at this early age, these boys can probably name two or three players they knew who were just as talented, in some cases more talented, but didn't want to make the commitment.

When I see the failures — and I've been seeing them for a long time — I know that the things people like Bum Phillips talk about are the things these players couldn't make themselves do. And in their other lives, away from sport, it's the same things that will always hold them back.

One of the roles of coaches is to be the players' conscience — to be, at times, their worst nightmare, demanding of them things they think they are incapable of giving. When everyone is giving them accolades, from family to the fan, and you're telling them it is not good enough, telling them they can be better, they look at you stupid-like. They think you're on something. How can everyone else be so wrong, and you so right?

But it's all part of the curve, part of the process of developing that talent into its full potential. A great American footballer named Otto Graham once said: "Everyone can't be the best at everything, but everyone can try to be the best at anything. If you give 100 per cent, you'll get your share of victories."

In telling a young player he is not going to make it — make it with us, anyway — for me one of the most satisfying aspects of the process is also telling him that you believe he did everything he possibly could to be a top footballer and he should have no regrets. It just wasn't to be. And it was nobody's fault.

Unfortunately, I have more interviews with parting players that I know — and they know — didn't give 100 per cent. They've become members of the "if only" brigade: "if only I had done this", "if only I had listened", ". . . if only".

Not everything is about winning, but instead doing the best you possibly can. As Otto Graham said, you'll have your share of victories. In sport, as in life, they might not always come when you want them. Still, they will come.

In 1997, when Paul Sironen won selection in the Sydney City representative side, I was so happy. Why?

Because I know the guy and I like him. Two years earlier Sirro was dropped from the Australian team and was in the twilight of a very distinguished career. On selection in that Sydney team, he made the point that he had decided to train a bit harder and to make some other sacrifices.

And, hey, he got the reward.

It just reminded me that age is not *the* factor for success — it's just how much you are prepared to give.

I keep going back to American football on this subject, maybe because they have looked at it longer and harder than we have, but one of their legendary motivators, George Allen, definitely got it right. Allen said: "Desire, dedication and enthusiasm are the things that dominate in life, whether it be in sport or the business world. If they can maintain those three qualities, they can have the things they want. They will have learnt a work ethic that will always make them employable and always sought."

The challenge for all these young men is to maintain those qualities. It's not complex. Sure, it can be helped by coaches and family, but always it will be up to the individual to make the sacrifices, to supply the enthusiasm and desire to be the best. To give 100 per cent.

We can all tell sorry tales about the guy who had it all but ended up with nothing, though I don't weep for him. The best quote I have read about all this I cannot attribute, but will borrow all the same: *We only fail because we give up trying.*

A RULE FOR HELPING PEOPLE

When you send out a player off the bench, you're not hoping for a miracle . . . that, maybe, he will do the job. If you didn't believe in him, he wouldn't be in the squad at all.

Unlike some people, I lose no sleep over such things. Why should I? Some people spend their wasted lives worrying about things they cannot change.

There's a rule to helping people: the one you are trying to help can't be fighting against you — first off, he's got to want to help himself.

I never want any team I coach to rely on one player. I'm not saying that doesn't happen, it's just that I don't want it. It's the team that succeeds, not the individual.

THE VICTORY IS IN BEATING YOURSELF

WHAT'S A GOOD LOSER? WHAT'S A BAD LOSER? IS THERE ANY such being?

Growing up around Warwick in Queensland, I'd listen to those who influenced me and to the mates I knocked around with, and I'd hear them describing this guy and that as "just bad losers". We might have been in a pool hall or on a sideline or in a backyard, but I never felt comfortable with them making excuses for individuals mouthing off and hitting walls, screaming and carrying on.

I was too young to challenge it too much then, but as I grew older I came to realise that these people carrying on were generally *good losers* — they actually didn't mind losing; some even planned for it. They were the guys who didn't put the work in and then they'd turn around and want to can everybody else.

The more I tried to find a balance between those who hate losing and those who don't, the more I realised the loudmouth was putting up a smokescreen designed to prevent people from realising that *they* were in fact behind the losing.

I have never accommodated too many of those guys in my sides.

Even at the Broncos in the early days I had directors coming into the rooms after losses, complaining that the players were not hurting enough.

"How do you know that?" I'd inquire.

"There's too much noise in here . . ."

"I saw one of them smiling . . ."

And they had, too. But it was never a problem, because some of the fiercest competitors I've known and coached didn't mind a bit of a joke after a loss. This has been the case down the years in football. In fact, Ron Massey tells a wonderful yarn from his days at Parramatta, when the great Mick Cronin missed an important goal, a sitter, in a vital game right on fulltime. Back in the losers' dressing room, when Mick finally appeared, The Bear,

Bob O'Reilly, lifted his head, turned to a team-mate and said, "Look out, here comes ol' Golden Boots."

What matters is what these people do in next week's match — not what they do straight after a game.

Players work it out pretty quickly, and we're all different.

One day we, as in the Broncos, lost, and Gene Miles will never let me forget our 40-minute ride home from the airport. Gene was playing back then, probably the captain, and he was driving. There was only one passenger — me. I just got in the back seat and never said a word the whole trip. Not a word. Gene says it's the worst drive he's ever had in his life.

Allan Langer and Kevin Walters were different again. Their way of handling a loss was to have a few beers and get into their mates. The bloke who had dropped the ball with the line wide open, Alf and Kevvie would tell him he had hands like feet. They'd grab at an imaginary ball, miss it hysterically then fall onto the ground. It might sound a bit odd but it worked — for them and everybody around them. It was relaxing, believe it or not.

If Wally Lewis had a bad game, or the team hadn't played well, he'd never say much. The champion competitors can be like that. But you see them at training during the next week and they really put in. To a winner, losing never comes easy.

One thing I absolutely hate about today is there's too big an emphasis on winning and losing. To me, it's the most false thing I'm involved with.

Over many years at the Broncos we've had some success, and that's important. It's good to win, but winning is the end product of everything else you do, not the be all and end all.

Steffi Graf used to say her greatest challenge was playing against herself, and I truly believe that, because you can do no more than your best.

Take that US Open quarter-final in 2001 between Pete Sampras and Andre Agassi: 6–7, 7–6, 7–6, 7–6 to Sampras. The greatest game you'll ever see. Does Agassi walk off and say, "I'm a loser"? Is Sampras so much a greater genius for having won an extra point in a marathon? Looking at most of the fans, that's what they'd have you believe.

Sport is about testing the limits of the human heart — your limits and your heart.

The thing about this winning and losing is that you can win and give a mediocre effort and you can still lose after giving it everything you have. I know which effort I'd be more proud of.

Sport is about giving it everything — that's how you learn. Often parents ask me about advice for their kids just starting out in sport. Apart from the obvious fun factor, I tell them to teach their kids to be competitors. Not to quit. Not to give in. To judge themselves not on what others do but on whether or not they've given everything.

Vince Lombardi, the great American coach, liked to speak about that feeling of exhaustion. He liked seeing his players lying there in pools of sweat, knowing they'd given everything they could.

I suppose giving your best is about duty.

Duty is the most esteemed word in our language. "Do your duty in all things," wrote Robert E. Lee, Army

General of the Confederacy. "You cannot do more. You should never wish to do more."

So back to the parents: teach your kids to be the best they can be. Teach them to compete – not to give in. Teach them to forget the scoreboard.

When we're on holidays, we get on the beach for cricket in the mornings and footy in the arvos. We get 20 kids lining up. I love watching the kids. We played the other day and there was this big guy, so uncoordinated, but he was trying his heart out.

I felt a sense of endearment to him. I know this guy can train day and night for the rest of his life and not reach what you call great heights because he's uncoordinated — but what he has is a tremendous attitude to do his best. I am always going to make sure he's on my team because he makes people around him on the beach want to do their best.

Obviously, I don't put a lot of credence in what guys say after games, particularly when they haven't played well. Just watch what they do through the following week and how they play the following weekend.

I don't think you can judge it any other way.

If you're fair dinkum, a real competitor, you know what Steffi told us long ago – that you have to compete against yourself. The people who compete against themselves are the real competitors. They don't come any tougher.

That's why most of us don't want to do that, because it's too tough. Why would you judge yourself against somebody else? Blowed if I know.

And the greatest challenge is getting the best out of yourself *every time* you go into competition. This is what defines the great players and the great teams, holding it together for much longer periods of time.

Look at Patrick Rafter — here's a guy who goes out and does his best, plays above himself. That's another difference between a winner and a loser: a winner is a loser only because he didn't know how or when to quit.

At day's end, if you quit, if you give up, you're never going to find out how good you really are. I know this paraplegic guy. He's a 50-metre swimmer, and he's been to two Paralympic Games. In the four years between the two Games he improved his time by 0.1 of a second. To improve by 0.1 of a second he worked out he had to do 4000 hours of training. So he did it. And he went from bronze to gold. One-tenth of a second.

He beat himself.

THE FALL GUY

WHEN FRIENDS RING TO TELL ME THEY HAVE JUST BEEN appointed coach, I always say, "Commiserations."

It's a bit like that: you chase the job and really want it, but the job has a lot of pitfalls. In two or three years they will have fallen out with everyone. Their wives and the fans, the committee, of course, and all they'll have left is, well, not much.

There's not much difference between the general manager of a company, an army officer or a coach. It is important they have a pretty strong will, know where they want to be going, are committed and not easily distracted.

Pope John Paul II said: "See everything, overlook a great deal and prove a little." I like that.

There is so much to see and do, and while you have to see it all, you can never do it all. Many coaches, they see the big picture but never manage to narrow it down to improve small areas before moving on.

As for being strong-willed, hey, the fans and the family, sometimes the players, they'll all be telling you what should be done. Start listening to fans, though, and it won't be long before you're over there sitting with them.

That's a key part, standing by decisions, being confident that you're going to make enough good ones. Having a plan, and changing it rarely. Poor coaches change it often.

The biggest mistake a coach can make is to not be himself, to be manipulated. You can have love affairs with players — and that's OK — but remain strong enough to know when they're using you up. People say I have favourites. I do. But they're all good players.

And that reminds me of the wag in the grandstand at a time when one of my so-called favourite players was well and truly out of form. The wag stood up, and yelled: "Bennett, why don't you do the right thing and marry his mum?" I liked that.

Look, if they're going to sack you, when you walk out the door do it with no regrets, leave with pride and self-esteem. If you listen to others, and let them manipulate you, they're going to sack you anyway.

No one can coach without discipline, but make too many rules and there are just more to break. Don't complicate matters, just give the players a framework not too fancy to work within.

And motivation. The unmotivated cannot be motivated. When I first coached and saw a player with talent but bad attitude at another club, a player going nowhere, I'd go for him. It was always his old coach's fault and I could turn him around. But I was wrong. It wasn't the coach, it was the player, and it just reminded me that wherever you go, you have to take yourself.

Coaches don't win, players win, and a coach is not as smart as people say when their team wins nor as stupid as they say when they lose. At day's end the trick is to improve the player, to have him playing at, or close to his ability.

In the NRL, the stark reality is there can be only one premiership-winning coach every year. The ones that don't win the competition can't all fail — and they don't.

There are two types: the coach that builds and the one out there looking for a quick fix. The quick-fix coach comes in, upsets everyone and everything, gets some results, but within two or three years his organisation is in tatters.

Ring some bells?

I love the coach who says: "I coached good but the boys, the bloody boys, didn't they play bad?"

Bear Bryant, the great American coach, wanted the respect of his players if not their love, and I can say when things have been bad my players have always supported me. As he once said: "If anything goes bad — I did it. If anything goes good — good, we did it. If anything goes really, really good — congratulations fellas, you did it."

For coaches, every year there's a period that I call "scrutiny time", when rumours begin and jobs often end. Sure, we ask ourselves why we do it. The coaching bit, that is. To experience all the lows in your life? Or is it just an adrenalin shot, keeping us hooked?

The former coach, now journalist, Roy Masters, when coaching, said he was a masochist, that being the reason he coached. A masochist is someone who inflicts pain on himself, and Roy Masters' explanation is still the best I have heard.

You know deep down that you'll get yours, too, in the end. The sack, I mean.

Yet you live in the belief that you will see the warning signs first and resign. But it rarely happens that way. It's not because you are afraid or unemployable that you stay — you genuinely feel that you are doing a good job with what's available as far as players, finance, the club . . .

But, of course, the administrators and, at times, the players, the fans and the media, they don't always see it the same way. Everybody thinks you would be better off coaching somewhere else — everybody except you.

Tommy Docherty, the soccer coach, reflected after his sixth sacking, "That's the nicest sacking I've ever had."

The fall guy in most organisations is the coach. It's a bit like replacing an out-of-form player. Sometimes you don't drop him because his back-up player is no better — so you stick with him and make him better.

The same people who appoint the coach are the people who usually sack him. The question to be asked here is if they believed he was good enough in the first place, where does that leave their ability to make such judgements?

Coaching has changed so much, even since I began coaching in the Sydney competition. The major problem for a lot of coaches today is not the game plan or the players but instead what happens outside the playing field. With commercialisation of our sport, the contracts and escalating payments, coaches are now much more accountable for the selection of recruits and the selection of the team, all the time having to sidestep interference from administrators.

The commercial reality, you see, is more pressure on them, the administrators, as well.

You are entitled to look at all of this as just a bunch of words, part of everyday footballing life, but to a coach who doesn't handle these outside influences properly, it means his job.

Coaching ability has always been about communication and the ability to gain respect, the ability to be single-minded. Now organisation is added to that, and the ability to control variables that weren't there when I kicked off.

The most difficult thing with coaching is that you have to rely on other people to make your career a success. So, crucially, you have to know people and be with those who want success for themselves and want to help you along the way. Winners. One hundred per cent people.

And if you can't recognise those attributes in people, then your time as a coach is ticking away, faster and faster. Tick, tick, tick . . .

STAND FOR SOMETHING

When talk turns to successful football clubs the discussion is not complete, there's no full stop, until mention of the Miami Dolphins.

With win No. 325, the Dolphins' Don Shula became the most successful coach in National Football League history.

Shula says of leadership: "The biggest problem with most leaders of today is they don't stand for anything.

"Convictions provide that direction. If you don't stand for something, you fall for everything."

However inadvertently, Don Shula has helped me. His favourite saying is: "Success is not forever — and failure isn't fatal."

He says once you accept that, there is the capacity to rebound.

MANAGING THE MEDIA

MY FIRST REACTION WHEN I MEET SOMEBODY IS TO BE WARY. Why? I just want to suss out who they are and what they are, that's why. As Bart Cummings, the grand old man of the Australian turf, said of his trainer son when he got busted for allowing vets to treat his horses with illegal drugs: "He's a lovely boy, but he can't pick 'em."

Picking 'em is not something you learn at university — no, you learn it at the school of hard knocks: who you can trust and who you can't. It saves a lot of disappointment later on.

If I feel I can trust you, then I'll be me. If I'm unsure, or feel that I can't, I'll stand off.

Apart from the ABC-TV show *Australian Story*, why nobody outside our circle has ever seen the real me is because, generally, I'm extremely wary of the people asking me the questions.

Those I do trust, they see a different person.

So when I go to media conferences, whatever, I go there with a whole lot of trepidation. I don't really want to be there — and I suppose my demeanour clearly suggests that. It's not an act. It's just how I feel.

The two happiest periods in my coaching life have been in 1987 with Canberra, where the role of my co-coach, Don Furner, was to handle the media (I just loved it), and the 1998 Origin series when I got the shits with them and had the no-talkies. I only talked to the media post-match.

During the 2001 State of Origin I didn't talk until the Saturday, at the last training session before each game, and I still remember my whole mood changing when I'd turn from the team to do what I had to do. In one turn of the body I'd go from relaxed and happy to apprehensive and defensive.

When I put a total media ban on at the Broncos later in the same year, well, that was one of the best times of all. My quotes weren't in the newspapers, I wasn't seeing myself on the TV . . . it truly was a beautiful thing.

Look, I'd talked to the press all my life.

My regret about not talking to the press those last few months of the 2001 season was that I couldn't give Wendell Sailor the accolades I wanted to give him. Big Wendell was leaving the Broncos for rugby union after giving the club magnificent service, excitement and greatly adding to our history.

To my eye, the media in the main has a negative agenda, they are always looking to find fault, while my life's been about positives, about giving people confidence and building clubs.

Some journalists don't want to do the research, don't want to put the effort in. Some are looking for a quick story without putting in a lot of work and they're looking to find fault.

Hey, I'm not faultless. And our organisation at the Broncos is not faultless. But there are too many in the media who want to find bad all the time and that contradicts what I'm about — I'm always looking for the good. The lies, the deceit, the bullshit, it's not something that sits easy with me. I've never wanted to play their game, whatever *their* game is.

This all goes back a long time, because I've been at war with them since I was a player. When I began coaching the press quickly decided I couldn't coach. At Brothers and at Souths in Brisbane they wrote me off. That's OK. But now they want to tell me I can coach. I didn't listen to them when they said I couldn't, and I'm not going to listen now.

During the Justin Hodges blow-up in 2001 — when I opted not to play Justin after he announced he was going to join Sydney City at the end of the season — the press decided because I wasn't going to play Justin in the Broncos side any more, it wasn't just me that was wrong but the whole ethic of it all.

Fine, they're entitled to their opinion. When I made the point that Justin showed no loyalty . . . how do I put this . . . the journos who were criticising me have never employed anyone in their lives. While the press was being so critical I was receiving faxes from employers, I had talks with people in the street, strangers, and from it all I picked up that the press' opinion wasn't widely shared. I am not saying I was right or wrong, I'm just saying the reporting of this situation looked a trifle unbalanced.

Wendell Sailor had given his all to the Broncos over nine years. He thought it was time, time for him to move, luckily while at the top of his game and by his own initiative. But he had given great service to our club.

In contrast, the gifted Justin Hodges came to our club at age 16 and was being groomed for a position —

Wendell's position. We'd spoken about 2002, and indeed everything we worked together on was about him being the Broncos first-grade winger in 2002. Then, by choice, Justin signed elsewhere for 2002. Good luck to him. He's just a kid, and I hope he goes a long way. Me, I had to educate a new winger and I was running out of time. You don't expect anything back, and sometimes you don't get it, either. That way, you're never disappointed. But we had to move on.

I admit that I go to press conferences and look at the people asking the questions and think: didn't you watch the game? I'm not saying you have to have played football to know football, because you don't. But it has to have been a part of your life for you to properly understand it. You need a passion for it. Football should not be simply a job to you. Not if you want to understand it. It should be much more than a job.

Again in 2001, what about the Brad Fittler situation? What a stinker that was. It epitomised the press to me. Some magazine mob framed a number of questions, one of which was name the three most overrated players in the game? They came up with Brad Fittler. For a week the back-page headlines everywhere — well, in New South Wales and Queensland, anyway — were based on the fact that Brad Fittler was the most overrated player in rugby league.

I've watched Brad Fittler since he was a schoolboy, seen him play for Australia, for his state and for a couple of decent clubs, captain them all, and you know what — not once have I ever heard him come out and say what a good player he is. In fact, my impression is that Brad Fittler has always handled himself with great humility.

So who overrated him?

Coaches, former coaches, press, so-called experts in the media, they all waltz around giving him huge wraps — and they're the same people who lined up to tear him down. It wasn't just *reported* that these nameless players polled had voted this way, it was in fact *promoted* for days. By the exact same guys who put him on the pedestal. You go and work that one out.

The first thing I always tell my young players is don't put yourself on a pedestal, and don't believe what anyone says or writes about you. The more notoriety they get, the more I try to be there to keep an eye on how they handle it all.

Because I've seen the after-effects on too many occasions. A player can be in a form slump and work his way out. But if he's in a form slump and copping heaps of criticism and he doesn't know how to handle the criticism he's going to be caught in that form slump for a whole lot longer. Again, I'm not saying players should not be criticised — I'm saying they have to know how to handle it. And because the weight of criticism can hurt a player, I believe the press make too many instant heroes and take no responsibility for the damage.

There are agendas. One of those agendas is to tear the Broncos apart. In 2001, we were going through a tough period, losing players to injury and losing games and down in confidence and, presto, there was the chance to put the boot in. As long as I'm coach at the club I'll never let them have control, no matter how much weight some think they carry.

I knew the only way to make some of them happy was to see me broken, and when they knew they couldn't break me they started on my players. Journalists were ringing up, saying, "Off the record, tell me . . ." I couldn't believe the slyness of it all. Personally, it wasn't worrying me, but when they began to have a go at my players, I said, "That's enough."

Another thing I can't believe is how many highly intelligent CEOs and champions of business put so much emphasis on how they and their businesses are portrayed by journos. How they react to criticism. How they don't seem to believe in themselves and what they're doing.

Kerry Packer has hardly ever talked to the media, and he owns most it in this country. What he doesn't own, Rupert Murdoch does, and he doesn't talk to them much, either. What does that tell you?

The media is in competition. It's about ratings and newspaper sales and advertising revenues. And shareholders.

I'm not that naïve not to know that the game needs the media's support and involvement, even if I can take or leave them. I also realise that media people have a job to do and I have a job to do and most of them will give you up to do their job. Which is fine. But the nasty side of me comes out when I see unfairness to the game and its players and I wonder, if you put the microscope on their own ethics and work environment, do you think we'd find any fault there? Honestly?

I love reading good articles. I love to see a story well researched and balanced. Not about myself, though.

Strange as it sounds, what's helped me deal with it over the years is how I've felt about myself. From the time I began coaching I've done the best I can, and if someone outside those I'm working with has criticised me, so be it; I'm doing my best and I know that.

But if Allan Langer or Kevin Walters or any other guy I respect criticised me, then I'd stop immediately, look at myself and take it all on board.

That's the difference.

WINNING

"If you do
what you always did,
you'll get what
you always got ..."

DON'T DIE WITH
THE MUSIC IN YOU

Entertaining the masses is something I've never tried to do, though privately I'm a great one for clichés, with favourite sayings and words. Instead of dropping them in the media, I prefer to keep them to myself, to my own thinking, though at times I'll share them with my players. To me, it's better to speak for five or ten seconds than to dribble on for five minutes without getting the message across.

Some go back to my times in the police force, like . . .

Isn't it amazing how much can be accomplished when no one cares who gets the credit?

A lot of people worry not about getting the job done but about who's going to get the credit. I've always said to the players: "Let's get the job done . . . and we'll all get some credit."

The media, like the fans, has its favourites. Some guys can just run on and be assured of a rap. Others, they might not be fancy, but they're players you know are valuable to the team and its spirit. They must know that you know their value.

A famous American intellectual, Oliver Wendell Holmes, once said: "Many people die with their music still in them. Why is this so? Too often it is because they are always getting ready to live. Before they know it, time runs out."

Don't die with the music in you.

That's a life of potential never reached, the fellow who never practised as hard as he should have, who never made the sacrifices, who might have been . . .

It means don't go through life, whether it be relationships, sport — life — sitting down at the end and saying it could have been better. No one is going to finish with a clean slate, having realised every bit of potential. Still, there's no reason why some slates should be so bloody dirty.

There are no great men — only great challenges which ordinary men are forced by circumstances to meet.

Often we hear the comment: "Isn't he a great man?"

Perhaps he is, perhaps he's done some great things. The assumption is he was born great.

I once read a wonderful article about Weary Dunlop, how when the challenge came he met it. Now they say what a great man he was. Weary Dunlop was, in fact, an ordinary man, but he met the great challenges where other people might well have walked away from them.

The most successful people I've met are the ones who handle adversity in the right manner.

For most people, two or three times a year in relationships or business they're going to face some high drama. Handled wrongly, the damage can be irreparable. The ones who handle it right solve it so much more quickly. They're the ones who get on with their lives.

The highest reward for a person's toil is not what they get for it but what they become by it.

So often the question is: "How much am I going to get paid?" When it should be: "What will I become by it?"

Accept criticism and disappointment as a part of life, and when it comes stand up straight, look it in the eyes and say you cannot defeat me — I am bigger than you.

Self-explanatory, as is my other favourite, a piece by Dale Winbrow, titled "The Man in the Glass".

When you get what you want in this struggle for self
And the world makes you king for a day,
Then go to your mirror and look at yourself
And see what that man has to say.
For it isn't your father, your mother, or wife,

Whose judgment of you — you must pass,
The fellow whose verdict counts most in your life,
Is the guy staring back in the glass.
He is the man you must please — never mind all the
*   rest,*
For he's with you clear up to the end.
And you have passed your most difficult and dangerous
*   test,*
When the man in the glass is your friend,
You can be like another and chisel a plum,
And think you're a wonderful guy,
But the man in the glass says you're only a bum,
If you can't look him straight in the eye.
You can fool the whole world, down the pathway of
*   years,*
And get pats on your back as you pass,
But your final reward will be heartaches and tears,
If you've cheated the man in the glass.

WINNING IS A HABIT

OFTEN I WONDER WHAT IT IS THAT BRINGS ONE MAN SUCCESS IN life and mediocrity and failure to his brother. The difference can't be in mental capacity; there isn't the difference in our mentalities indicated by the difference in performances.

In short, I've concluded that some men succeed because they cheerfully pay the price of success. Others, though they may claim ambition and desire, are unwilling to pay that price.

These words, and others, were sent to me this week by a Broncos fan. They originally belonged to Herbert F. De Bower, and they got me thinking. Winners, I know, aren't born, just as no one is born a loser. It's what you make of yourself.

Something I always find fascinating is how sporting critics determine who is a winner and loser, because, as I've said before, I don't necessarily agree that you have to win all the time to be a winner.

In the United States I heard about Bill Parcells, then the coach of the New England Patriots. They'd been losing for a long time before he arrived, and straight away he took them to the playoffs.

Parcells walked in and told them: "You must take yourself wherever you want to go. The point is, if you're in a losing club or losing team, you have to be a part of the problem." What Parcells was saying is: you can't blame everyone else.

In life or football you either buy winners or you make them. By winners, I mean people like big John O'Neill, who played in eight grand finals for Souths and Manly between 1965 and 1973. Wherever he went, he made winners.

People like Glenn Lazarus and Mal Meninga. Wherever they go they take an attitude, a winning one, and it pays off.

Take Wayne Harris, the Melbourne Cup-winning jockey. Through brain-tumour operations, brutal falls and weight problems, he just wouldn't give up.

All this is true in reverse, with certain groups and individuals who never win. There are people who make others play worse, who hold them back.

Manchester United, Liverpool, Herb Elliott ... winning is a habit but, unfortunately, so is losing. Anyone can have a bad trot, but bad trots don't make losers, they just make you die a little. By keeping together a group that has had a fair bit of success, you've always got a chance.

The problem comes when you have a group that has never known or been associated with success. So when you get with the right people, you might not even notice the change in your habits, but it's happening.

If I ever begin to accept losing, I'm out of the coaching caper. I can live with being beaten and understand that if the team loses an individual can still feel OK in himself because he played well. I suppose a guy who doesn't play well but is in a winning team can feel good for the team, but I wouldn't, not if I hadn't made a contribution.

In our game winning starts on Monday, but for boxers with just four fights a year or swimmers who peak but twice a year, winning starts much earlier. If swimmers stand on the blocks and know they cheated on a push-up or a lap three months beforehand, they're prepared to lose. When a winner fails, he trains harder while a loser blames others. When a winner makes a mistake he says: "I was wrong." A loser says: "It wasn't my fault."

A winner feels responsible for more than his job. A loser says: "I only work here."

"There ought to be a better way to do it," says the winner. Loser says: "That's the way it's always been done here."

There is no greater tribute in sport than to be called a winner, especially when you've known the feeling of a loss.

FLEA-BRAIN MENTALITY

I know this fella in America, he plays out of left field. Goes to Country Fairs, see . . . walks in under the arches and heads straight to the flea section. Forget the clowns, the elephants and the merry-go-rounds, this fella is always headed towards the fleas.

For ages he just stood there looking at them jumping up and down in glass canisters. The fleas don't jump out, ever, even though the canisters have no lids. Finally, being an inquisitive fella, he seeks out the flea trainer.

Flea trainer says, "It's all in the way you start with them."

Huh?

"Well, you put 'em in the jar, whack a plastic lid on it and the new fleas begin jumping up and down, bashing their little flea-brains on the top. After enough headache experiences, they stop jumping quite so high and settle in their comfort zone. It's then that I'm in a position to take off the lid and they'll be contained in that jar forever more — not by a lid but by a mindset that says so high and no more."

In football, we have all suffered concussion, been knocked out . . . but some of us still haven't had enough headaches to give up. Some of us still want to jump . . . higher than high.

As Bryce Courtenay wrote: "If you're skating on thin ice, you may as well tap dance."

WHO DO YOU LISTEN TO?

I ONCE RECEIVED A LETTER THAT MADE ME THINK OF A LOT OF things I had perhaps been taking for granted. Big things, too, like self-esteem.

The writer, a former footballer of considerable flair and gifts, told of how at different times in his life, his self-esteem had been so low he really couldn't appreciate the accolades and recognition.

Shoot me for taking self-esteem for granted. It's just that the lack of it is something from which I've never suffered.

But, sure, I see it in others. When you see or hear of a great talent wasted, if it's not through bad attitude, the money's on it being through lack of self-esteem.

My understanding, or at least interpretation, of self-esteem is how you feel about you, and I remember somebody once saying no one could make you feel inferior unless you wanted to. The guy who can't handle a compliment, who's always looking for the ulterior motive to it, he's lacking, and in him I see elements of all human characteristics.

You sometimes want to grab him shake him — and say: "Look, don't you understand all the wonderful qualities you possess?"

Look at the positives that make you, and stop dwelling on the things that, at day's end, mean and count for nothing.

Self-esteem, as I said, is how we feel about ourselves. Part of that feeling can be given to us by others: that's precisely why we have to be careful in choosing the people with whom we surround ourselves.

It's a question I often ask my younger players in particular: who do you listen to?

Everybody gives so much advice to people in the spotlight, from social issues to finance and, of course, football. While you can't stop that and wouldn't want to, one of the things they have to get a grip on very early is who to listen to and who to ever so politely ignore.

In the letter, the guy explained how his coach had told him certain things he knew to be right, but he instead listened to others contradicting what the coach had told him. Well, he made some bad decisions, didn't he? Years later, in his own heart he realised the right and the wrong, and the bringers of both tidings. The coach had told him he was a good footballer but he had to be patient . . . Others told him he was better than good already, so in Lord's name, why wasn't he playing in the top grade?

End result? He walked away from the game at age 20, kicking the ground instead of a football.

I've found, whether by accident or design, that I can take advice from everybody but rarely will I use it — never unless it comes from an achiever.

By achiever, I don't necessarily mean someone who has scored a mountain of tries or kicked a few goals. I don't care what path they've gone down, so long as they've done the walking. That way, you know that they know the consequences — the price.

People who know those things rarely talk rubbish.

A STRANGER CALLED DISCIPLINE

RAP, SOUL, BLUES AND COUNTRY. CHAKA KHAN AND SLIM Dusty. Hey, Tina's got a new song. Weather reports, stock reports, sport reports ... politicians and piranhas drinking at the very same trough.

I'm flicking through the stations on the car radio when this vaguely familiar voice says, kid, get your cotton-picking fingers off the dial and listen to what I have to tell you.

Maybe not in so many words, but, suddenly, this guy has me riveted.

He's telling about his growing years, how he was bullied at school. Overweight and picked on, the brunt of all jokes. How he sat down the back, the class dunce. The school dunce. Just a dunce. Couldn't play sport, and couldn't do much else.

Flat out walking.

Then it happened. In 1963, the day he joined the police force as a cadet.

Talk about change, because at the Police Academy he met a stranger called discipline, and from that meeting he learned self-discipline.

Within a few years he'd played in a football grand final and not long after he had two premiership medals on the mantelpiece.

The guy telling the story was Rex Hunt, the VFL great who's better known in Queensland for kissing fish and calling that other game on the radio. And Rex was speaking for all of us regarding the need for discipline in our lives.

Discipline — and this is important — is not someone telling you to jump and you asking, "How high?", because a man convinced against his will is of the same opinion still.

It's self-discipline that counts. Whether a coach, a parent or a real friend, they cannot possibly know how much you love them if discipline is not part of the relationship.

When Rex Hunt speaks at schools these days, which he does often, his address is always directed at the kid down the back of the classroom, the one sitting there hiding some immense talent; whose effort and direction is wasted. Too often that kid is sitting there waiting for someone else to pick up the ball and run with it for him or her.

No matter how much enthusiasm the teacher has for you, or how persistent your family and friends are, at day's end it is up to you to be disciplined and motivated. If you love what you do, you can do anything. The flipside reads: if it's just a job, you're pushing shit uphill.

Discipline also means a no-nonsense attitude. That is, tunnel vision. Because the only lasting form of discipline is self-discipline. It's not like a tap that can be turned off and on. From your personal life you carry it into everything you do.

Bob Knight, the legendary and mad-as-a-meataxe US college basketball coach, admits it has always been his thought that the most important single ingredient in athletics and life is discipline.

"I have many times felt that this word is the most ill-defined in all of our language," says Knight. "To me, it means:

1. *Do what has to be done;*
2. *When it has to be done;*
3. *Well as it can be done; and*
4. *Do it that way all the time.*"

Through my involvement in sport and life, discipline has never been a *thought* — because I have always known it. Rex Hunt simply put it into words.

ARE YOU A HEN OR A PIG?

ONE DAY I WAS HAVING A CONVERSATION WITH ONE OF MY players, and he said: "Coach, I hate the feeling I've had this week."

He knew losing was part of sport, and he could handle that, but what he couldn't handle was knowing he had not performed as well as he could, that he had let himself and others down.

"I just hate the feeling," he said, "that goes with not giving your best."

There is no better way to approach your sport than the attitude of giving your best, regardless of the scoreboard and circumstances, the cheers and jeers. Sometimes I think this type of player is in the minority, most players being happy to sit back and wait for someone else to make it happen. Always doing enough to keep their position but never enough to be the difference.

I suppose the difference is that one is *committed* and the other is only *involved*. It reminds me of the ham and the egg story: the hen is involved, but the pig is committed.

A lot of people don't and won't make a commitment. Why? Because commitment means sacrifice and an elimination of excuses, it means doing away with rationalisation of your position and justification of your behaviour and performance.

So many of us like to be involved but not committed. Commitment means you have to strive for perfection.

Sure, you might not get perfection, but you will get a lot closer by committing to your dreams.

It means having no fall-back. No reserve position. It's 100 per cent effort, 100 per cent of the time.

Winners — and this probably best sums it up — make commitments; losers make promises.

Vince Lombardi said so many good things that publishers fill books with them, but one of the best was: "If you will not settle for anything less than your best, you will be amazed at what you can achieve in your life."

Commitment means struggle. It means effort. Always sacrifice and, at times, disappointment.

As the player recognised, it's the only way you can live with yourself, be true, by doing everything you possibly can.

Robert Louis Stevenson said it for everyone to hear, if not listen: "Sooner or later, everyone sits down to a banquet of consequences."

ATTITUDE MAKES THE DIFFERENCE

WHY? SOMEONE WITH SO MUCH OBVIOUS TALENT, WHY DOES HE choose not to make the most of it? Then there's the flipside: the lesser talent, but with *attitude*, sitting up with the champions.

No way is the first guy prepared to pay the price for success. For him, there will always be excuses and short cuts and quick fixes. The second guy, he just keeps on truckin'.

Victor Frankl spent the whole of World War II in a concentration camp, no excuses, short cuts or quick fixes. During this horrid time, his wife and only son died.

On his final days before release, at war's end, he was still asking why some gave up while others not only survived but grew stronger. Victor Frankl concluded that it was how people chose to perceive their experiences — their *attitude* made the difference.

The greatest discovery of my generation, and I read this somewhere, is that a human being can alter his life by altering his attitude.

Constant reinforcement is the key. Where do you get it? By spending time, every day, every week, listening and reading and mixing with positive people.

We can all learn from people who have turned around their lives. I have a book here called *Never Give Up*, and it is a good book, carefully stacked alongside Michael Jordan's *I Can't Accept Not Trying* and biographies of Muhammad Ali and Winston Churchill, Fred Daly and Weary Dunlop.

When trying to develop a better attitude, it's important to keep away from people who continually knock what you're trying to achieve.

Small people do that, while the greats make you feel like you too can become one of them. Hey, if you can't keep away from small people, just teach yourself to ignore them.

Ask yourself these questions:

- Am I allowing my life to be governed by daily activities, or do I choose to live in accordance with good principles?
- Am I allowing my life to be governed by outside forces?
- Am I so busy putting out fires that I don't have time to start any?
- Do I have important goals and dreams I am committed to, or am I creatively avoiding commitments by filling my life with daily activities?

Attitude is something you see by actions, not words. One thing I do know: most people these days know what to say and when to say it — but it doesn't mean they have a great attitude.

It's infectious, and the difference between good attitude and bad attitude is everything. At some stage, we're all going to face obstacles, and in many cases those obstacles will be ourselves.

For anything worthwhile, a price has to be paid: there needs to be, as Vince Lombardi said, planning and preparation, sacrifice and self-denial, effort and hard work and persistence and perseverance. To many, these are only words, and they're the ones with the bad attitude.

People with good attitude live by them.

Sooner or later, everybody sits down to a banquet of consequences.

CONFIDENCE BREEDS WINNING

*I never blame myself when I'm not hitting. I just
blame the bat. And if it keeps up, I change the bat.
I know that sounds silly but it keeps me from getting
down in the dumps when I'm in a slump. It keeps my
confidence up.*

— *Yogi Berra, Major League baseballer.*

JUST RECENTLY WE WERE DISCUSSING LOSS OF CONFIDENCE, OF
performance, when a coaching friend said: "You don't
know where it (confidence) comes from, or where it
goes to."

So many talented players have failed to reach the
heights because they did not have it. Confidence, that is.
Yet with it, I have seen just as many over-achieve.

Confident people realise their shortcomings but,
because of their confidence, work not just around them
but with them to succeed. It's about believing in yourself.
How can others have confidence in you if you don't
believe in yourself?

To players lacking a little on confidence I say: "Every
time I pick you in first grade, I'm giving you my
confidence." In every player I have picked for first grade I
have been confident, even though some of them were
not. They look at you. Sure, you can point them in the
right direction, encourage them, but at day's end it is not
up to you.

Confidence can be shattered by injury, by failure, by negative thoughts and by success. *Success?* With success comes other people's expectations, and often the recipient begins to change things about himself or herself.

When I came back to coaching in 1984 at Souths in Brisbane, Mal Meninga certainly wasn't playing as well as I knew he could. He lacked confidence. Simple as that. His attitude was still great, he trained very well, yet everything Mal did on the field indicated he lacked confidence in himself. Soon I realised it was because he'd played State of Origin at age 19, made Kangaroo tours and goodness knows what. Suddenly, he couldn't climb over the expectation.

Throughout it all I remember saying to him: "When you were 18, and just kicking off in first grade, what were your expectations?"

Mal said that his only expectation was not to let himself down. "I never used to think very much about playing until match day," he said. So I asked him to go back to those simple goals, to the way it was, and forget about everyone else. Every time he got the ball, Mal Meninga didn't have to score. Nor did he have to save a try every time they had the ball. Anyway, Mal went back to eating chicken sandwiches on match days and got through the next decade quite well.

Just the other day I spoke to one of my younger players who had just played Origin. He brought up the subject of other people's expectations and I went straight for the jugular. "I don't want to hear that again," I said, "and I'll tell you why . . ."

One thing we all have to do to help with confidence is learn to relax, don't ask too many questions. There is no special psyche, nor set formula for reaching our potential. Confidence is all between the ears — good and bad. Either you believe in yourself or you don't.

One of the things coaches, managers, parents, businesspeople, whatever, fail to recognise is that the majority of people need time to develop confidence. You must be prepared to invest that time and recognise it in the individual.

Take Steve Renouf. The first time he played in the top grade he dropped so many balls. Later, I discovered that his parents had come to watch him play, and whenever his parents came to watch he dropped balls. So we had to work out how his parents could come to games and he could catch balls all at the same time. Happily, we did. It was a similar story with Steve's defence, in that he didn't have the confidence to make the tackles he should have been making. With a little help, he built that confidence.

As people reach new heights they obviously grow in confidence.

Once at a function I did something right out of character. This top sportsman, right, I'd followed his career and like everyone else knew he had been going through a tough time. I just grabbed him and said: "Look, I don't want to buy into your business, because I'm sure everyone is offering advice. Others even want to change your technique . . ." After a short conversation this guy assured me the only problem was an injury.

"Great," I said, "you'll be back on top soon." In his mind there was an obvious reason, you see, for the form slump — like Yogi Berra with the bat.

Never put doubts in their minds.

I look at Doug Walters, the former cricketer, and notice he is different in that he enjoys life more than most. He made it work for himself. I've seen great footballers who weren't great trainers and been very wary about tampering with what made them great in the first place. One of my favourite sayings is: go back to what got you there — you're never going to be too far off the mark.

Confident people don't need to fear failure. It has been suggested that confidence is developed by practice. *Proper* practice. Improper practice gives you nothing but false confidence.

Our players and our children and our associates, they all need good feedback and not someone always homing in on their imperfections. I'm really big on never putting yourself down, on account of the fact others do that for free.

Some of the wise folk of sport have spent lifetimes wondering aloud about this subject.

Pro golfer Hubert Green said: "Winning breeds confidence, and confidence breeds winning." How true. If you don't believe in yourself, you're always looking for the negatives in others.

A quarterback in American football, some guy called "Tittle" of all things, once said: "You have to have a past history of some success to give yourself status and self-confidence. You have to have accomplished something before you can believe in yourself."

And once that confidence is there, don't let others shatter it. Building it is a process, a long process. It's not like building a house, where you simply pick the bricks and timber. It's more complex because, as my coaching friend said at the very beginning, you don't know where it comes from.

OUR GREATEST CHALLENGE IS OURSELVES

I WAS CHASING COWS ONE MORNING ON MY MATE'S FARM, wondering what would happen if I ever caught one of them . . .

You think the strangest things, chasing cows. Like the note my daughter once came home from school with. She'd been listening to Vicki Wilson, the Australian netballer. Vicki had said: "If you always do what you've always done you'll always get what you've always got."

I liked that one so much I took it to the players, reminding a few I'd been a little tough on lately that they have to change, because if they don't, they will never get better, never reach the heights I believe they can.

There's always room for improvement — it's the biggest room in the house. Clichés. Win without boasting, lose without excuse. Don't brag, for it's not the whistle that moves the train.

That's a good one when you're winning.

There's another: the bigger a man's head gets, the easier it is to fill his shoes. Ain't that the truth. But not everyone wins.

The other day I wrote this to a friend in jail, a footballing friend. He'd asked me for some thoughts to help him through a pretty tough time, and I didn't need much paper.

"A 'no' uttered from the deepest conviction is better than a 'yes' merely uttered to please, or, what is worse, to avoid trouble." And then I put in brackets: "If you had said no mate, you wouldn't be where you are today."

I rarely take much notice of critics or criticism, not unless it's justified, for the majority of critics know not victory or defeat.

To borrow from Theodore Roosevelt: "Better it is to dare mighty things, to win glorious triumphs even though checkered with failure, than to rank with those poor spirits who neither enjoy much or suffer much, because they live in the great twilight that knows not victory or defeat." Go Theodore.

Go Nelson Mandela, too. He spoke on one of my favourites, forgiveness.

"The weak can never forgive," he said. "Forgiveness is the attitude of the strong."

Mr Mandela also got it right about the fact that we can never forget, but must forgive, especially sitting opposite your adversary.

Some 99 per cent of failure comes from people who practise the habit of making excuses. So many coaches around the world have echoed the words of the NFL's Chuck Noll: "We tell our players that if they are going to point a finger, to point it at the mirror. The attitude has to be, 'If we're not winning, it is my fault.'"

I, too, have been to too many staff meetings where it was someone else's fault. And I've had more trouble with myself than with any other man I've met.

In my life, I notice a lot of people advising others how to run their lives even though they haven't got their own act together. Our greatest challenge is ourselves. Until we master ourselves, any words in the direction of helping others are worth no more than what I just put my foot in, chasing cows.

KEEP GOING UNTIL THE SIREN SOUNDS

IMAGINE YOUR TEAM BEING FOUR POINTS DOWN WITH 10 minutes to play, and walking off for an early shower. You storm into the dressing room with the obvious one-word question, Why?

"Because it got too tough out there, coach."

Too tough!

There was a time, when speaking to a group of kids, when they told me how they'd come home early from a camp. Turns out they had not exactly been staying at the Sheraton Mirage. So they'd had a committee meeting and decided it was much cosier at home in front of the fire with their doting families.

I immediately felt for those kids, because they had missed one of life's great opportunities to develop character simply by sticking it out when the camp got tough.

So often nowadays we let our young people down by not challenging them with situations where they can find inner strength; by leaving them in their little comfort zone.

City kids, particularly.

Another young person, but from the Darling Downs, told me a completely different story after spending days picking up sticks in the paddocks when the floodwaters had receded.

He spoke of the mundaneness of it all, but when asked whether he had got anything out of it, he smiled and replied: "Yes, I did.

"An appreciation for what I have. That, and that things don't always seem so bad."

Smart kid.

Negative comments about physical education programs in our schools always fascinate me, some people honestly believing sport and its many physical challenges deserve no role in our education system.

As we grow into adulthood, it's true, the enormous challenges are often mental and not physical, but are we not better prepared by the knocks and bumps of earlier sporting endeavours?

During one recent season, I was on the hammer of a certain Bronco, and in the end figured he deserved some sort of explanation. Finally, I told him that I had never learned anything from anybody who had not demanded more of me than I thought I could give, than I had inside me. The player then related the story of his years growing up, how his father was always giving him what he considered to be impossible tasks.

His dad was and is a farmer, a very tough man, who wouldn't accept "no, can't do", and today the player says it was the making of him.

The last time his father told him to go and do something was no different from all the other times in that the kid didn't think he could achieve it.

But a determination not to fail had been slowly instilled, and this last time he was out there for four long hours, refusing to give in.

"When I got home with the job done," said the player, "Dad couldn't believe it. He just looked at me. And, you know what? He never asked me to do another thing."

It takes courage and determination to keep fighting when you're down and all appears lost.

As I told that group of kids from the shortened camp, almost every successful person I have ever met could not remember anything great he or she had achieved without, at some stage, having wanted to turn it up and quit.

They might have been in the office, out in the paddocks or on some cold sporting field and felt like going home to sit in front of the fire. But they didn't. What they did was keep going until the siren sounded.

That's the difference between the success and the failure, not being smarter or having more opportunities, as some others will tell you.

Those who won't take risks and go for it, who won't see things out, they're the ones who come home early, never answering the challenge and never going anywhere.

Being courageous requires no exceptional qualifications, as John F Kennedy once remarked, no special combination of time, place and circumstance.

It is an opportunity that, sooner or later, is presented to us all.

WHAT "PERSEVERANCE" REALLY MEANS

I'm a big fan of the Tour de France. Great race. One of my favourites was Miguel Indurain, who, the first time he rode the Tour, finished ninetieth. The next year, he finished 40th, then 19th, then 10th . . . on form, you would have wanted to back him the following year and sure enough, home he came. And he kept on winning for five years straight.

Within Indurain lies the one message we all tend to overlook: most of us have highs and lows, it's the perseverance, the determination, at day's end that makes us what we are.

As I've said many times, many athletes compete not against other nations or team-mates but against themselves. In coaching, the most satisfaction I get is seeing guys who really had to persevere, overcome setbacks, finally achieve.

Perseverance, to me, is not about doing the same thing over and over. Just maybe you have to change, look at yourself.

It's a bit like fishing: after an hour in the same spot without a bite, sure, you can keep on sitting there. On one hand, that could be called perseverance: but, on the other, it could be called idiotic. Pick up the rod, son, and go down the beach 100 metres. Go on, be a devil.

Go for gold by all means. But if you don't find it the first time, take a look around or at yourself, then maybe dig another hole.

Ray Kroc, the guy who founded McDonald's, got it right a long time ago. "Nothing in the world," according to Kroc, "can take the place of persistence. Talent will not — nothing is more common than unsuccessful men with talent. Genius will not — unrewarded genius is almost a proverb. Education will not — the world is full of educated derelicts. Persistence and determination alone are omnipotent."

Not everyone in sport can win. For some the only prize can be the character they have built within. It can also be the greatest prize of all.

YOU'RE NOT A FAILURE UNTIL YOU START BLAMING OTHERS

EXCUSES, EXCUSES . . . SEVERAL TIMES DURING A SEASON I AM asked to talk to a group of young people delicately balanced between being kids and being adults. Some are only 14, others 16, and all have had difficulty fitting into the school environment.

A few characteristics have emerged in our talks, the stand out being the ability to make excuses. It matters not whether it's their parents, teachers, peers or police, yep, they always seem to have someone else to blame.

I have found these talks hard yards, often feeling like grabbing a few of them, shaking them, and saying, "Keep blaming others, and nothing will ever change for you", because, as Vicki Wilson says, if you do what you always did, you'll get what you always got.

For people so young, I can't believe life can be so complicated — I thought that only happened when you got married and kicked off coaching.

Excuses and alibis prevent us from being accountable, from taking responsibility. Sure, it's part of our nature to blame others, but if you keep going down that road there can be no destination. Just road. Before the beginning of every football season you could sit down and write the excuse scripts for coming losses: injuries, bad calls by the ref, tired, stupid, a whole lot of other theatrics.

At the Broncos we have been together long enough for me to speak on behalf of everyone when I say that we don't make excuses. If we had been playing football as we should have, we would not have been in a position where a call could settle the game. It was our fault the score was so close, and we can't blame anyone for the loss.

We don't go for the injury bit, the sick bit — we win or lose. That's all. As Sam Rutigliano, the college football coach, said: "A man can make a mistake but he isn't a failure until he starts blaming others." Wait, there's more. "Success is simply a matter of luck — ask any failure!"

It's not a case of worrying about how tough the challenge can be, it's a case of proper preparation, focusing and practice. You alone are responsible, and if you can accept that about yourself you can begin being a winner.

To the kids I say: "OK, I realise some of you may not have had pleasant experiences but, at day's end, nobody cares what you're up against." And I tell them about the American coach who never told anyone he was sick because 80 per cent don't care and the other 20 per cent are happy.

Ah, Americans. What about Al Davis, who owns a lot of things, from big gold necklaces to the Oakland Raiders? He said: "Just win, baby, just win the game."

For these young people, like the rest of us, the game we really have to win is the one of life and if we can't accept responsibility we lose, our family loses and the team ceases to exist. If people keep trying to help, and you keep looking for easy ways out, after a while nobody cares.

A MATTER OF PRIDE

"I AIN'T NEVER HAD MUCH FUN. I AIN'T NEVER BEEN TWO INCHES away from football. Here, guys go fishing on the day of the game, hunting, golfing and all I want to do is be alone studying how not to lose."

These words belong to Bear Bryant, but I can so easily relate to them, especially on weekends after a match.

Some people collect stamps, some butterflies and others wives. Me? I collect quotes.

Bill Parcells, one of the American football's coaching greats, is always good for a line, the one topping my list, with due apologies, being: "Don't tell me about the pain, just show me the baby."

I use this strictly in reference to footballers, not mothers. Too often you hear why something can't be done when the more natural thing is to just go and do it.

Henry Ford made cars and billions of dollars. He also made for interesting reading. "Anyone who stops learning is old, whether at 20 or 80," said Ford. "Anyone who keeps learning stays young. The greatest thing in life is to keep your mind young."

And it is, too.

More of Ford's words ring out in these times of change in our game. He said: "If money is your hope for independence, you will never have it. The only real security that a man can have in this world is a reserve of knowledge, experience and ability."

Makes you want to go out and buy a Fairmont, doesn't it?

Another good one for these times belongs to Harry Truman. "It is understanding that gives us an ability to have peace. When we understand the other fellow's point of view and he understands ours, then we can sit down and work out the difference."

Oh, there is another Truman saying, which I use at home: "I have found the best way to give advice to your children is to find out what they want and then advise them to do it."

How, well, true.

I don't know who "ambition is enthusiasm with a purpose" belonged to, but I don't mind pinching it from time to time.

Often people try to make our game so very complex and get the great things mixed up with the not so great. However great, it remains a simple game and Maxwell Maitz got it right when he penned: "Nothing is more simple than greatness. Indeed to be simple is to be great."

Talent is God-given, be humble. Fame is man-given, be thankful. Conceit is self-given, be careful.

So many quotes ring true about the very same things. Like Dwight Moody's "I have had more trouble with myself than with any other man I have ever met" and Sheldon Kopp's "All the significant battles are waged within the self".

One of the great mistakes is to measure yourself by what you have accomplished, rather than what you should have accomplished with your ability.

One of my favourites belongs to golfer Nancy Lopez.

She said: "A competitor will find a way to win. Competitors take bad breaks and use them to drive themselves much harder. Quitters take bad breaks and use them as reasons to give up. It's all a matter of pride."

RUGBY LEAGUE

"It's not
always about
scoring more
points ..."

LOOKING GREAT WITH
YOUR JUMPER ON

OFTEN WE TALK ABOUT HOW MUCH RUGBY LEAGUE HAS changed, particularly in the past 25 years. The role of many positions on the field has changed as dramatically as anything, but the great characters still epitomise their respective positions.

No better place to start than the front row.

Without front-rowers and their ability to do a job you can't have a football team of any quality. The first thing every club boss in every country town will ask when you walk in is: "You wouldn't know where we could find a front-rower?"

I believe this position is the toughest to play. Twenty-five years ago, they were simply the enforcers of the game and, I guess, to a lesser extent that is still part of their job. But stiff arms, boxing matches and softening-up periods have been replaced by sustained, aggressive defence and power hitting — all within the rules.

Front-rowers have to be very single-minded. Often they don't possess great speed and in most cases, no great evasive skills either. So whether the team wins by 50 points or loses by two, there is still no easy way out for the front-rower.

I think the great ones had a lot of character about them. Take Arthur Beetson; he had tremendous mobility and tremendous skills. Great hands. He was one of the greatest because Arthur had that little bit more.

When I say front-rowers are different, you only need to have followed the careers of people like Martin Bella, big Blocker Roach, Sammy Backo, Shane Webcke today . . . but I suppose one of the endearing characteristics about the majority of front-rowers is that they always engage their mouths before their brains.

They're classics. Once on tour in New Zealand in the 1980s, someone made a reference to all the sheep there and Blocker said: "Yeah, you can get as much pork as you want here!"

Sammy Backo. Ah, Sammy. We were coming home one night and the pilot informs us we will be 15 or 20 minutes late into Brisbane because of a very strong headwind. As we were coming into Brisbane, the pilot returns to say that he's been able to increase speed and we'll indeed be arriving on time.

Sammy turns and says, "Coach, it's a good thing that headwind was with us."

Sam Backo is still trying to work out how come everyone dies in alphabetical order.

Second-rowers. I can't say a lot about second-rowers. They're like 1000 lifesavers. They are very dependable guys.

One position which has really changed is hooker. When I played, the hooker's job was to get dummy-half, to pass and tackle.

The modern hooker is more like a halfback of 25 years ago. They would all be fine halfbacks but not great halfbacks, lacking just a little flair. Still, they're cheeky like the No. 7s, usually tough too.

Locks. Now here's a role that has changed. When you talk of great lock-forwards, the names John Raper and Ron Coote spring to mind. But it's different today because the lock no longer has to cover defend. They're usually tall, rangy, with great pace and clever with the ball.

Traditionally in this game, if your lock is OK and your halfback is OK and your five-eighth is OK the team is better than OK.

Halfback. I have never coached nor seen a good halfback who wasn't cheeky, and I sometimes worry about that characteristic. The halfback is the catalyst of all things, on and off the field.

If I go to recruit a halfback and he's not cheeky there's not a bit of rogue about him — I tend to drift away. Again, I think his size makes him what he is. He's been a bit of a dwarf since childhood, the butt of a lot of fun and jokes, so his personality has developed around that.

Five-eighths are usually good steady types of people, often the steadying influence on a club. The great ones, because of the sacrifices they have to make for the team, are great team men.

Centres. Tremendous speed and flair, and can be prima donnas.

If Chris Johns had any prima donna in him, Kevin Walters knocked it out early by throwing him terrible passes and having him knocked out. I believe the hardest place on the field to defend.

Wingers. This position has changed more than most. Once they were purely finishers, waiting for the ball: now, with all the kicking, they are much more involved.

I think the fullback has to be mentally tough. He's in the situation where everyone sees every mistake he makes. A lot of the time he has little or no control and if he dwells on his mistake, he's gone for the rest of the game.

Lately, I have noticed many more athletes coming into our game, but coming into it without football sense. Footballers know where to put the ball, they know where there's a gap, how to read a game — but the athlete knows none of this.

The things I talk about, the know-how, it has been learned in the backyard.

If we're not very careful and we trade the football instinct for athleticism, the game is going to get pretty boring. The other guy can run all day and looks great with his shirt off, but he plays pretty dumb.

As my mate says, you can't put brains in monuments.

YOU'VE GOT TO TRY SOMETHING

The more I see the way a lot of coaches are coaching the more I'm convinced that outside of being a good athlete not much is required of today's players.

It worries me because I think we're getting to the stage where kids are over-coached. We're producing more guys capable of playing first grade but they're not passing, not taking risks, and I don't think it's improving the standard of football.

Obviously a player still has to be able to catch the ball, but a lot of teams seem to go for the big and strong, with good mobility. He gets to the advantage line and invariably dies with the ball. They're yardage runners, they can tackle and they can get the job done.

An old coach up here in Brisbane, Bob Bax, a great coach, once said to me that if a guy comes in with a stats sheet that's all clean, he hasn't been doing much. He's been taking no risks. Assume he's tried nothing.

I like to see a bit of flair, the unpredictable, particularly when I first see a player, the ability to run and pass and take an option.

It might not always be the right option, but he's got to be trying something.

Don't get me wrong, you don't want a side full of space cadets. If he's been in the NRL for a long time and is still taking too many risks, you're not going to refine him. But if he's a kid from the bush, he's the one you want.

To be a first-grader he has to be a good athlete; even the small guys need super strength levels. He must have good speed, even the front-rower. It might not be how long it takes him to cover 100 metres, it might be 10 or 15 metres, the ability to move laterally, to play the ball quickly.

Then he has to be able to handle the grind.

The first few times you shave, when you're young and just growing up, it's a great thrill. But when it's every day, a bit of a chore, that's when attitude counts.

Two guys I brought here to the Broncos, they both thought they were ball players. One guy came to grips with if he did it the way we wanted, he'd play first grade. The other guy? He's someplace else now.

NO WORK, NO PLAY

FULL-TIME PROFESSIONALISM IN SPORT SOUNDS, WELL, professional. It's an issue I studied long before the salary boom in rugby league: an issue on which I've very strong opinions.

Footballers differ from Olympians in that our game is contested every weekend for up to eight months of the year, whereas Olympians set themselves for only three or four events a year. Olympians train rigorously twice a day and genuinely need plenty of rest in between. If they're not training, they're sleeping or eating. They have neither the time nor the energy to hold down a real job.

Several times I've been to America looking at gridiron and its full-time professionalism. Been to the UK looking at soccer, too.

Because of their strong work ethic, in America they make the players fill up the whole day studying: things like videos of themselves and their rivals. "Xs and Os", as they call them. From eight in the morning to four in the afternoon, six days a week, they train physically only once a day. Don't worry, there's lots to fill their days.

I've been in those classrooms and the players who aren't asleep owe it to copious amounts of black coffee.

The coach? He just keeps talking.

Like with most staff meetings, they eventually walk out with all the problems still existing but the boss always feeling better.

In the UK I saw some contrast. At one club the players come in at 10 o'clock, have no lectures, train, and are home at one. Every day.

At the other club I visited they come in at nine, go through the classroom stuff, the videos, lunch together and train in the afternoon. At three, they bundy off.

Sure, I asked the coaches: why? One said he worries like anything what his players might be doing afterwards. After knocking off, he roams the clubs and bars, driving time and again past the all-night parties praying not to see a familiar face. Another coach worries about his players' insular lifestyles, that they don't mix with anybody bar footballers.

No one works their hours, and because they don't mix, they could get very bitchy, inward: the little things invariably becoming mountainous issues. It's not unlike people who never leave a small town. Born there, die there. They think they know everyone's business, yet on the world scale of things they know little.

Anyway, I came away from those situations determined that full-time professionalism was not for me or my players. I find little value in being able to play sport but not life. In the US National Football League there's merit in the college system because the players have some kind of degree and life skills behind them by the time they turn pro at 22 or 23.

Those apprentices in English soccer, that's sad. Some as young as 16, hoping to make it against all hope. They get bundled out of the system at 19. I'm sure they can still kick a ball, but suddenly there are no goalposts, and their only chance of a career is a car out of control.

Look at the kid in Australia who quits school at 14 and nine months. He's 45kg. He's going to be the next Mick Dittman. By 18, he's 75kg. His old mates are at uni, his new ones are riding in races against Dittman. He's sitting in the stands, the public stands, with no job and not much else.

We have a greater responsibility to our young players than to promise them all glitter, and deliver no more than a grunt and a door with "no entry" on the other side.

Sportspeople don't live in the real world. They have managers running around for them, people rubbing them down, spit-polishing their boots, doing their banking, generally sorting out their problems. So comes the day their playing careers are over. They're 30. It's not easy to grow up at 30, and even as full-timers I doubt we could train one more minute than we do now, not when we play every Sunday.

To me, the ideal situation is for the established players to work three or four hours a day, just enough to get them out of bed.

Younger players we encourage to get careers, to work their eight hours a day before training. Whether they be at college or doing apprenticeships, you'll see them turning up come May or June looking very tired.

We have a policy at our club concerning younger players. No work, no play. A lot of these kids turning up tired, they're not going to make it in football but, as I tell their parents, we don't want them to be failures in life.

Players have to get away from football so when it comes time to play they're looking forward to the game, the contest. We want them stimulated, not sour. We want them out on the street facing up to their public when they've played both well and badly. It's never a bad thing for them to face the music rather than hide behind the classroom doors with their robot team-mates.

There can be no guarantees in our game, and while I see the younger players questioning the outside work requirements I still rest knowing some of the most talented kids I've ever seen never made it.

I have a friend whose 15-year-old son only ever used to come out of the surf to go to school, eat and sleep, and at times he didn't even come out for that school part. He got offered a job a couple of afternoons and Saturday mornings at $4.50 an hour.

By the time he'd paid his bus fare from school to work and home again there was only small change, and the boy questioned the job's value.

His dad said: "One day you'll understand, just get on the bus."

The old man's right: "Just get on the bus, kid, and enjoy the ride as much as you can."

TURNING RIGHT

To my mum, the "turning point" in football is when she gets to the intersection closest to ANZ Stadium, sticks her arm out the window and carefully steers the old Vauxhall hard right.

It has become one of the hip sayings of the modern game, the journalists sitting in the stands with the headline *Turning Point* awaiting them in the computer back at the office. The game was won the moment this happened or that happened. Every week everyone seems to know before me exactly where the games are won and lost.

Take one of modern football's finest games, Origin I, 1994, and *that* try in the 79th minute.

In rugby league terms it was a great try incorporating everything you want to coach. With the clock running down, the first thing Queensland did right was what they didn't do — panic. Instead of hoiking the ball madly from one side of the field to the other in search of a miracle, they looked to two big forwards to go forward in quest of better field position.

More importantly, they waited for their backline to be set for one of those moments magically mirroring all those years of practice and drills.

Desperate yet controlled, Willie Carne knew his pass had to go over the top, and that he could throw it one-handed, on to Steve Renouf, whose juggling act with the ball we'd seen a thousand times in training at the Broncos.

With practice, there needs to be little or no thinking.

Thinking, with practice, transforms to instinct.

No way did Renouf have to think about catching that ball. He just caught it, like he had been practising.

Renouf and Michael Hancock hadn't always been able to find one another, to link, and it had been a great frustration to me at times. Yet here they were in the single most desperate play of a desperate match, linking like brothers. Instinctively.

Renouf — Hancock — Darren Smith, they all drew their respective men before what was the critical part, involving Langer, Meninga and Coyne.

Mark Coyne had been involved way back at the play-the-ball where Meninga was the dummy-half and Langer the first receiver, and all they did was stay alive, heading straight downfield.

I thought Coyne did an absolutely remarkable job in getting the ball down. Here was a player totally aware of the situation, smothered by two defenders and caught short of the line.

Once I read an article headlined "Flow", about the mind being in total control of the body. I looked at Coyne as the fulltime sounded and thought: "Flow, Mark Coyne — and welcome to the magical moment of your life."

At night's end, though, it was not the only turning point in the match: the first came at no single moment but for the opening 25 minutes of Queensland's defence. NSW had scored on them and were coming back, cavalry style, trumpets and all, to score again and had Queensland not held out, they were gone.

The second turning point came with Carne's move to fullback after Julian O'Neill got hurt. With clever and daring positioning, Carne played the most vital role in Queensland's two late tries: the one for 12–10 by keeping the ball alive as he was going to ground, getting back to his feet and figuring again in the movement.

But perhaps it was a third turning point — unnoticed by most — that meant more than any of them. It had to do with NSW's elation at the Brad Mackay try for the 12–4 break. Every NSW player on the field, right through to the bench, acted like the crackers were going off on New Year's Eve. When I saw those Blues jumping up and down on the bench, to me, that's just about the worst thing you can see in football.

Their actions stated: "Hey, we can't get beaten now."

If I had been the NSW coach with a walkie-talkie I would have given them the biggest rev-up ever. No I wouldn't. I would have gone down to the bench, right along it, and anyone who jumped up I would have knocked down.

That kind of stuff is for after the game. When it happens during a game you know they are thinking: "We've got this, I'll just ease up, drop back a gear, make certain I make no mistakes and hallelujah, we can't lose."

The problem is, your 12 other guys are saying the same things, and suddenly everybody's focused on the outcome and not the next six tackles.

It's never the one thing that kills you. If you've done everything well from the kickoff you don't have to worry any more about the last 10 minutes than you did about the other seven brackets of 10. A silly penalty, a dropped ball, a lack of desperation — they count the whole time through.

So that try might not have been the turning point, but it was verification of Queensland's uncanny ability to create something from nothing under the greatest pressure.

It's what wins Origin games, wins Tests and premierships. Two points behind, two minutes on the clock, everything's riding and the players respond.

We don't just coach to see that, we live for it.

It is the basic reason little old ladies keep turning right into ANZ Stadium when they could just as easily go left in a dark cloud of smoke.

THE WAY OF THE DOLLAR

A MAN'S TREATMENT OF MONEY IS THE MOST DESIRABLE TEST OF HIS character. How he makes it, and how he spends it. At the moment there's a bit of money, more than a bit, around sports, so let's try to add up a few of the misconceptions.

I once read where Andy Haden, the former All Black turned players' agent, said we must realise that the game of rugby now belonged to the players and the fans. But he was wrong on one count. The games — and I stress *games* — now belong to the players and the corporations.

Where does the fan sit? In the stands. He has no control any more. A stranger who happened to read this story walked up to me and said a pretty sensible thing, how the fan lost control the day his or her admission outlay no longer covered the wages of the players.

In 1995, the Australian Football League did a survey on this very topic, and according to them the guy in the corporate box was already greatly subsidising the bloke in the beanie downstairs. It cost the average fan $11.60 to get into the Aussie Rules, whereas it costs the game $26 to have him there.

Money, to me, is not the problem in sports. Already we have seen amateurism, whether it be the Olympic Games or world championships, take your pick of the track-and-field meets, cycling, go the way of the dollar.

Great professionals are even competing at Commonwealth Games and we're seeing dramatic change in rugby union where their whole motto once rode on playing the game for the love of it, that and for their team-mates. Money had nothing to do with it. It has all changed now, though.

The problem we face is how to handle it, both individually and as groups, because success has made failures of many people. In AFL and rugby league, where there have been fair incomes for a number of years, we have some experience in handling the financial situation but in rugby, well, the code is in for some difficult times.

I look overseas, to American football, ice hockey, basketball and soccer, and no matter the mountains of cash they still produce champions and high standards of play.

People say choose a job you love, and you'll never have to work a day in your life. I'm with those people. And I don't believe players in the future will falter because of huge incomes.

The two major problems with money . . . greed runs first by a mile. Look at basketball and ice hockey in North America, the strikes about their pay, and remember they're not striking about the first million dollars but the fifth and sixth they want to make a season.

The second part? The fan.

They're the people you don't want to alienate. While he or she might not be paying the total bill, I would hate to go to any contest where there is no one in the stands except for the corporate boxes. Fans create the atmosphere so important to players. You could argue horseracing continues to prosper financially despite the fact the stands are empty, but while the horses undoubtedly prefer the peace and quiet, I'm sure the jockeys don't.

More than ever I sense the fan doesn't resent what the athlete is paid so long as he or she is not taken for granted. The fan smells greed a long way off, and if the wages go up and the performances go down that's what they resent.

The risk in team sports is the guy who plays one year too many just for the money, the pay packet. He's out there hiding, getting so much and giving so little.

Ask someone who is sick what they most value, and every time they will say their health. Money never gets a mention. I remember Paul Hogan during the Los Angeles earthquakes, saying how he would just pray he would be OK, that all the money he had accumulated could not get him out of those ones.

Always competitors must endeavour to maintain the attitudes that made them play the game in the first place: the enjoyment, the dedication, tenacity and perseverance that made them stars.

The money comes along only as a reward. If the competitor becomes complacent, or satisfied, it's goodnight from him and goodnight from you, money being a terrible master but an excellent servant.

In my playing days — and this is something I have forbidden as a coach — it was not rare for a well-heeled supporter to come into the rooms before a big match and offer us $500 a head to win. The team would invariably go out and play terribly. I realised then, and still do, that money is not the main motivation in sport because if it was we would have won those games.

It's only important when you sign the contract, when you are doing the deal, but when that's over it should not matter and with the great majority it does not matter.

In the mid-1990s at the Broncos we had a boy, well short of his 20s, who had received an offer of a huge amount of money from a rival organisation. In a conversation with our general manager and others I decided we would not even make him a counter-offer but instead let him go. He's gone. The story here: I just felt if he stayed at our club he would be staying for the wrong reasons.

I also believe that at such a young age he should be worrying about where he's going instead of arriving somewhere, and if he's going to go to the highest bidder now, he's most definitely going to go there a few years down the track anyway.

I'll tell you what I worry about in regard to money and sport. I worry about the guy you need in the team, the guy who is not a superstar, yet his contribution is just as great. You know the superstar, he's always going to be courted, but not the guy who might have missed out on a bit of grace but no grit.

One thing you cannot coach against is the fact that some of them will finish their playing careers with nothing to show for it except their scrapbooks. They make poor business decisions, waste enormously, but there's nothing you can do about it and I find that very frustrating.

There are two ways to get enough. One is to accumulate more and more, and the other is to desire less.

A MAROON OBSESSION

As THE WEATHER COOLS ABOUT ORIGIN TIME, I FIND THE BEST way to warm the feet is to place them not in front of a log fire, but instead before a white-hot newspaper headline.

I can cop the State versus State, mate versus mate and even family versus family bit. Honestly, though, passions can border on the ridiculous.

For the best part of a week during Origin '94 (I wasn't the Maroons coach that year), I was in Armidale on the New England tablelands, where the mountain mists announce winter and feuds are not between the Martins and the McCoys, but between New South Welshmen and expatriate Queenslanders.

It's halfway along the back road between Sydney and Brisbane and newspapers are trucked in from both the north and the south.

One that I picked up screamed: "Maroons blunder". And I thought: oh my God, what have we done? Shock. Horror. Reading on, it turned out Queensland had picked no ball-playing forwards.

So I looked at the other team and I didn't see any ball-playing forwards there either. I thought about it a little further and realised that at the time there were only three ball-playing forwards in the competition. We had one of them at the Broncos, Terry Matterson, and he wasn't playing in the upcoming Origin match. Neither were the other two.

Again I relaxed, feet as warm as toast. Just as I was feeling comfortable I picked up another paper and there it was: "Maroons not split".

Don't tell me my Broncos in the Queensland side have all been fighting, I thought, but reading a little further it was revealed that Tosser Turner had assured everybody they've never been more harmonious.

On the Broncos' final training night together our centre, Chris Johns, came up and said, actually he kind of whispered it: "I'm really keen about playing for NSW, but Kevvie (Walters) and Alfie (Langer), they're just obsessed about playing for Queensland, aren't they coach?"

I say: "Johnsie, it's been that way since they were born."

Soon as NSW go into camp Kevvie would be on the phone, at dawn, telling Johnsie and Glenn Lazarus (our other guy born in the south) all the gory details about what Queensland are going to do to them.

One of the big things for an Origin player is to keep his sanity — and the more he plays, the saner he becomes in this circus. You'll see the first-timers going gaga, getting carried away. That's one of the reasons the selectors tend to stick with proven campaigners.

When a NSW team chasing a series hat-trick was announced it was obvious they had followed a Queensland tradition in rewarding those who had served them well. Loyalty can at times be fraught with danger but I can see the logic in it.

We were sitting together when the Blues side came through and, while excited for Lazzo and Johnsie, a couple of my guys commented on different NSW players who were out of form but still got picked.

I made the point that by the faith and confidence the NSW selectors had shown in them, they had just said: "Look, no one ever writes you a letter but the player is smart enough to realise he's back because of the way he performed last time. He knows what's expected. It's a tremendous motivation for him personally. He knows what he has to do to be picked again."

I can understand the passion. Listening to the informed people of Armidale, it's the women, you know, the *women* who want to see them fight. People not normally interested in football become very emotional. It changes people.

I met the craziest Maroon supporter, married with three children. The quietest little guy you've ever seen sitting there next to his wife, holding her hand.

She told how she got scared when Origin time came around, the moment he strutted into the loungeroom in his Maroon jumper and switched on the TV.

When Queensland score, he'd jump up and tackle a bag he had strategically placed in the corner. A fight breaks out and he's into it, madly punching at shadows on the wall.

It gets to a crucial stage and he ups and throws himself backwards over the armchair.

I looked at the guy — this nice, law-abiding citizen — and I said: "Is this true?"

He looked at me sheepishly, paused and replied: "I'm afraid it is, Mr Bennett."

YOU'VE GOT THE WRONG ONE!

In the early years, before the Cowboys, the Broncos played several games in Townsville against Sydney clubs. We have always been extremely well received up there.

It was in Townsville, for such a match, that I first met Gorden Tallis. He was no more than 14, still growing, when he appeared out of the night as the players were doing their warm ups.

Walked straight up. "My name's Gorden Tallis," he said. "You've got my brother, Wally, down there."

I said: "Yeah, we do."

And he said, bold as brass, before disappearing: "Well, you've got the wrong one, haven't you!"

THIS IS WHAT MATTERS THE MOST

OPERATION SUCCESSFUL, BUT THE PATIENT DIED. THAT WAS certainly how I felt straight after the final of Super League's Tri-Series in 1997, a match NSW won after a remarkable contest that was finally decided after more than 100 minutes of thrilling rugby league.

The game itself was obviously the successful part, reminding us that all the hype and marketing doesn't mean a great deal unless the product is right — and the product was great.

And the greatest satisfaction? No spite, just tremendous passion and toughness.

All that is good about the game of rugby league was brought to the surface.

There were moments, sure, that could easily have been whirred into controversy, but the game consumed it all, and in the end everyone forgot the tough calls and the wrongs to get it right.

A friend wrote to me in the week after, the way a friend writes to you when there is a death in the family. It was that sort of game, highly emotional, and at the head of any subsequent conversation your friends are never sure how you are feeling.

The letter explained how the guy sitting next to him at the game turned around with five minutes to go and said: "I don't give a stuff who wins — this is the best game I'll ever see."

To create such a game there must be two teams, and NSW, whatever we did, they were just as courageous and talented and gifted.

As a coach, I've always felt my job is to coach and the players' job is to play, and we don't need all the pre-match controversy and hype about the fact we're going to have a great game on our hands. The greatest thing we can do is prepare properly and play flat out and let the rest look after itself.

You don't need to be on drugs when you're in football because there are no higher highs or lower lows.

In that Tri-Series final, so many things happened to confirm the toughness of sportspeople, and I'm not talking just physical toughness. To play so well and do so much only to finish second is a matter for mental toughness.

If you can't handle coming second, well, then it becomes even tougher.

We didn't talk much after the game because it had all been said on the field.

The only thing Queensland didn't do was win. The look in Allan Langer's eyes, the glare. The only thing that gave up was the scoreboard.

I did say to Alfie, and to the team, that he was a magnificent captain who had led from the front, but to never forget the 16 players behind him, following and leading at the very same time.

I also reminded them that while you can't take away the disappointment of losing there is a self satisfaction about doing your very best and, in sport, that's the thing you have to come to grips with — finishing second.

There will be days when you win but haven't done your best, and no way should you feel good then, either.

One of the senior players walked up in the rooms and said: "Coach, I feel OK about it." And that is exactly the way he should have felt.

It is important to be together at these times, as a group. The shrinks call it Group Therapy, and now we know what they're talking about, though we haven't got around to holding hands just yet.

My parting words were to do with my immense pride in them. And I told them I knew Queensland would also be very proud of them.

That seemed to mean the most.

GRAND FINAL DAY

SUNDAY TOO FAR AWAY. GRAND FINAL DAY IS SUCH A SPECIAL occasion for the players, for everybody involved.

The unseen if not unsung heroes of this are the families of the players and officials. They make a lot of sacrifices throughout the season and know how important it is on the big day for their husbands and sons. It's a great occasion. When you've done a lot of things in football, played first grade and represented a bit, above it all it's these grand finals that kind of make it seem and feel worthwhile. It's an emotional time.

I know in my mum's case, when we played in those grand finals she refused to listen to the radio or watch TV. No one was allowed to ring her.

Mum would wait till five o'clock and put the radio on, but only briefly. It was the only way she could handle it. It can be very traumatic.

What do I miss most when the Broncos aren't there? The event. That special feeling in the week leading up. It's what you've trained for. It's just about everything.

From Saturday morning on, after that last training session, the hardest part is the wait.

You just wish to play it at nine o'clock in the morning.

So when you get on the bus it's not far away, and the rest just clicks into place. It's virtually routine now.

Anybody who says playing in a grand final and winning isn't one of the best feelings of all hasn't won one.

It's the ultimate. It deserves every accolade, and I don't think there is a word or feeling that can overdo it.

The one thing that struck me in grand finals, or after them anyway, there's this reflection on the enormous amount of sacrifice and work which has gone into that one performance and you know the game's not really won on that Sunday afternoon.

Go back to November, to December, the previous January or February, to that torturous hill some trainer found or the outback ground with no fans and no cheers, just self-sacrifice and a determination to get the job done.

Go back to the sheer exhaustion, to asking yourself: is it worth going through all of this for that one final moment? And then, two weeks later, it's over and you're having to look at the next one.

That's why some teams and some guys never go back and play in grand finals, because they don't get it out of their system. They're still living on and for that one afternoon in September.

And, of course, there is a great danger for the losing guys as well, because they sit there asking themselves: why have I nothing tangible to show for it?

So they spend the entire off-season asking themselves: was it all worth it?

You'll notice in the lead-up to a grand final that players will explain how they've learned to publicly treat the big match as just another game of football. You know it's not, but everything has to be in perspective. If you put any more emphasis on it it'll just blow you away.

It's double-dutch, or coach-talk, saying something when you know something else to be true, and it's ridiculous to think it's just another game, because it's not. But to make it into a bigger event, when it's already so huge, that's a psychological blowout.

By taking the other approach, the momentum of the week will hype the players but it will be controlled hype.

Once on the field, however, more than anywhere else, it is just another game with play-the-balls, running and passing.

Players might look back and realise they'd played in tougher games, and I think Mal Meninga said exactly that after the 1994 grand final, but they've got to be ready to accept that. If it comes easy, take it. Whichever way it comes, just be ready for it.

When you win, no, I'm never happy for myself. Feelings vary with different coaches and different philosophies, but the first time we won I just felt very lucky, very humbled to have come from Queensland country with no special qualifications and be part of a Winfield Cup grand final I'd only dreamt about a decade before . . . to be part of it with such a wonderful group of men.

The best part, or feeling, is the family. They believed all along and suddenly don't have to put up with the smart alecs and knockers, not for three or four months at least.

You're never going to shut them up forever but there is no comeback with a grand final triumph, and that is a glorious feeling, particularly for family and friends.

All of a sudden you don't have to go around justifying your players and your club to anyone.

In life, if you're going to do or say something, first of all make sure you're a winner.

After the game, the win, you go around that stadium and come home through airports and realise what it means to people, you feel happy for them.

A lot of people live their winters, their lives, through football, you see it in their faces, and that is what makes it such a passionate game. I first saw it in State of Origin, and sensed it at Souths in Brisbane, where everything seemed so small compared to what happens in the NRL premiership.

TEAMWORK

"Spirit is built out in the middle ..."

WHEN SOMEONE'S DOWN, ANOTHER PUTS IN

A LOT OF PEOPLE PREACH TEAMWORK BUT PRACTISE MISTRUST AND selfishness. In teamwork, the leader — whether it be the coach or the captain or the army guy with whatever ranking — the most significant part is that he practises it too.

The old adage about a champion team always beating a team of champions says a lot but it doesn't say it all. For one, there's nothing in there about how to build a team.

Wherever there's a group of people involved the first thing is to all work together, get on, in the understanding that the team overrides the individual. No one will ever jump up, say: "I'm bigger than the team."

Still, you're always looking at their actions.

The guy who believes he can't be done without, who figures he should be the centre of attention, who's selfish or full of himself, he's the one who ignites power struggles. In power struggles, people take sides. No one wins. So at the first opportunity you move to eliminate the problem.

It's about ego. There's nothing wrong with ego so long as it's healthy, one which promotes confidence but still allows its owner to be part of the team, one which promotes leadership even without the captaincy, yet realises the owner is not indispensable.

One guy full of himself, and the team's in trouble. Two or three? You're no chance, particularly if the guys have high profiles, commanding a fair bit of respect outside the game.

He won't share. At halftime, when he knows his mate's tired but he still can't pick up a drink for him on the way through. He gets asked for a lift, knows it's out of his way, says: "No, I gotta get home — see ya."

The little things, they erode away at the team.

As I've already stressed, honesty is the other thing they must have. One of the great sayings the Americans came up with is: "I goofed." I made a mistake, in other words. Players — anyone in a group situation — if they can't say that, they are without honesty.

They need common goals, week-to-week objectives and the realisation that when the team has success they all get rewarded.

Teamwork can't happen overnight; it has to be developed, built in time. When the Broncos came together in 1988 we had a lot of great players but we were lacking.

In their second year, the coach of the AFL's Adelaide Crows, I read somewhere, took his players away and one of the things they did was walk over hot coals. One of the players got his feet burnt, and I remember the criticism at the time.

I knew what he was trying to do. At the Broncos we haven't done the hot coals bit but we have been to army camps, been put in horrible situations of adversity and found out who wouldn't carry the drinks at halftime, wouldn't offer the lift and would seek the soft option.

John Kennedy, the great Hawthorn and North Melbourne coach, once said: "In the faces of the greatest adversities the game can promote, each and every member of the team must know he can depend on each and every one of his team-mates not to let him or the team down."

I've had some tremendous experiences in my coaching career epitomising the making of a team. In the Brisbane competition in 1985 we'd been through some tremendous adversity and, six weeks from the end, were playing at Redcliffe in a match that would have a major bearing on the semi-finals. We put them away late in the game. It was such a tough match, awesome, and when it finished I knew we'd win the grand final. They knew it too, more importantly. I said: "You're going to win the grand final." They just looked at me, too tired to talk.

Same with the Broncos a few matches from the end in 1992. A cold Friday night out at Penrith, one hell of a football game. It was not spectacular, just tough, and we got up on the bell. I told them that night too, that they'd win the grand final. We had been five years building. When someone was down, another would put in.

At different times the team will struggle and often someone will say: "Let's go out and get on the drink." But I've never felt getting on the drink with team-mates builds too much spirit. It might not do a lot of harm, but it's not the answer. It solves nothing. Spirit is built out in the middle.

I try to avoid rules. I believe the perception is that I have just two: I'm always right; and if I'm proved wrong, rule one still applies.

I have, in fact, three rules: be on time; when I'm talking, give me your attention; and train and play flat out.

THE SPIRIT OF THE SOLDIER

Football's a tough old game, but alongside war it is not even kindergarten. I think if today's players had to do it, they would. Still, it's a question they'll never have to answer.

Not many long-generation Australians have not been affected by war, whether it be fathers, grandfathers, great uncles or aunts. As a boy I still remember buying the Anzac Day ribbon at school, clutching it, and comprehending its values.

It is a spirit we, as a nation, must uphold and prolong. The freedom of our country is something to celebrate, just as the diggers who gave it to us are to be honoured.

I remember going to Adelaide, a city boasting a beautiful war memorial. Beauty seems a strange word when related to those who have died for their country, but it's the word that came to mind when I visited alone.

Looking down the lists and lists of names, you search for a Bennett, and finding one, even knowing you weren't related, you're left wondering about the guy, somehow proudly.

IN THE END, HONESTY PREVAILS

Sheep are cute. Sheep are beaut. Sheep are soft
and curly.
But when I take them into town, I have to set off early.
'Cause they never go the way I want, so I need someone
to help me.
I just give a whistle, and call for Bob the Kelpie.

BACK IN SEPTEMBER '94, DON SPENCER'S SONG, *BOB THE Kelpie*, was my son Justin's favourite.

This I remember because between the time Steve Renouf was cited on a Monday during that season's semi-finals and cleared on the Thursday night he played it, top to bottom, precisely 549 times.

I found myself at training with quite a serious mob preparing for a sudden-death semi-final and in grave danger of bursting into song about cute, beaut, soft and curly sheep and a dog named Bob.

But that, of course, was not the Broncos' lone concern that week. Look, I didn't take a real lot of notice of the tackle, not at the time. I remember Steve Renouf coming at Manly's Jack Elsegood at great speed, skidding, his body peeling off to one side at the last minute. Out of the corner of my eye I saw it flash up on the big screen. I turned to watch it again, quite comfortable in the knowledge that knees in the back are not the go of Steve Renouf.

It wasn't until after the game, during the press bit in the corridors under the stadium, that I thought of it again. A couple of journos were probing about it, and I thought: "Here we go again . . ."

I went straight back into the rooms, straight to Steve, and asked him about the tackle.

"I didn't mean to hurt him," he said, adding that he didn't think there was much in it, definitely nothing to worry about.

I said: "That's fine. If you did nothing wrong, we've got nothing to worry about."

Next morning the papers led on the tackle and I thought, oh yeah, pretty typical. But then the bells went off like the whole city was on fire. The League general manager, John Quayle, rang John Ribot, our chief executive, to inform him that Steve Renouf had been put on notice for a possible citing. We had never received a call like that from Phillip Street, never heard of anyone being put on notice. So Ribot rang Frank Stanton, his counterpart at Manly, and Stanton said he hadn't viewed the tapes nor spoken to coach Bob Fulton about the tackle.

By the time I got to training Steve had been cited. He looked relaxed, and I was too. So I just said: "Gotta go down, eh mate?"

He said: "Yeah, I've got no control over that." Again he explained the tackle to me, "instinctive" being one of the words he used.

At our place, there's always plenty of geeing up, and one of the half-dozen of our guys to have been cited and subsequently suspended earlier in the year, said: "You're gone." Another said: "Three months!" Renouf said he didn't care whether he copped three weeks or three months, that he knew he had done nothing wrong and that was all that mattered to him.

We had a team meeting where I told them I thought Steve would be cleared, that we could not allow it to affect our preparation for our upcoming match against North Sydney. At training on Tuesday I again grabbed Steve to ask him how he felt. Relaxed, he said, and I told him to keep it going that way. On Wednesday we had a meeting for an hour and a half with our solicitors, just tying it all up, and then the word came through about the prominent football guy walking around Sydney saying, no, explaining, that Steve was going to get three or four weeks.

I did what I always do in these situations headed bush, straight to my mate Ged's farm with my son, the *Bob the Kelpie* tape blaring away. We were sitting down to dinner before leaving for home, and through 7.30pm and 8 o'clock when the phone rang a few times, my mate would say: "That'll be the news on Steve."

I told him I didn't want to hear it, that my way is to lock it out. I'd prepared myself. Michael Hancock was going to be in the centres, Paul Morris on the wing.

Anyway, the calls had nothing to do with Steve and we set off on the 90-minute drive. Justin's listening to the tape and I'm thinking of my last words to Steve: "You've got to go in there prepared to lose, because if you go in in that position, then you can't lose." And a tick before nine, and after a considerable debate on the pros and cons of survival without *Bob the Kelpie* for just a couple of minutes, I convinced my son to pop the tape and switch on the news.

It led the bulletin — Steve Renouf cleared!

I pulled up and gave my son a big hug.

He appreciated it, even though he didn't understand what it was for, and moments later as he sat back and started humming to the music again I wound down the window and started barking and whistling to the bush.

I felt a bit emotional, which is not something I easily admit. Cane me for being corny, but I've always believed in this country, that honesty prevails in the end. For the remainder of the drive I reflected on a season of ups and downs, of tremendous adversity at different times . . . the hard decisions.

What I came up with was the quality of the young men with whom I work, young men with an ability in most cases to accept responsibility for what they are and what they represent. All week, Steve Renouf had looked at himself, and, like the rest of us, liked what he saw.

People underrate the effects on an individual of such things as public citings. Just recently I was talking to a group of schoolchildren and telling them that before they did something silly, they should think how it would affect others.

One said: "Yeah, but if I do something silly, I'm the one who gets punished."

I suggested he have a think about that, about his mum and his aunties and uncles, that maybe in certain cases others were left to carry the scars.

THE FEAR FACTOR

COURAGE, IN RUGBY LEAGUE, IS NOT BLINDLY OVERLOOKING fear, but seeing it and conquering it. It's a thing we seldom discuss as a team or in life itself.

But in body contact sports there is no doubt players require great courage.

Fear, or the inability to conquer it, is one of the major reasons many young men don't play body contact sport. And sport can be dangerous to body and limb.

Often you see analogies between war and sport when, in reality, they cannot be compared. In one there is the possibility of death. But in sport, while there's injury, a combatant can get off if he or she wants, they can back off. Take their ball and go home.

Physical intimidation is a big part of our game, and it's true the fear factor is not often talked about. You'll hear the comment that that guy doesn't like body contact, or this guy's playing a bit scared when in fact all footballers are showing enormous courage just being there. It's just that certain others have their fear factor under greater control.

All players fear. In the change-rooms you see the different signs, some guys dry-retching, other guys sitting in corners so apprehensively, their stomachs churning.

Once the ball's kicked off, though, and he gets knocked over, the worries usually pass, unless it's a particularly bad start to a game, a confrontation, say, he loses, and then he'll take more time to adjust.

The worst part, the greatest challenge, is definitely the wait, whether it be in the dressing room or the trenches.

That's why after a game we sense so much self-satisfaction from those players who met the challenge, who overcame the fear. Still, the same contest is going to be there the next week, and the week after.

When I coached at Canberra in 1987 — and this was part of my development — I remember frowning upon myself for never having spoken to players about courage, let alone fear. Earlier, when I played, I felt I never had the courage of some others, and didn't consider myself as *tough* as they were in this department.

When I gave away playing, I finally talked about it and soon realised that in just playing the game I had passed the greatest test. I could have played other sports, but doing what I did each Sunday, tackling the fear, made me feel so alive. Worthwhile. If I hadn't met that challenge I would have lost self-esteem.

Anyway, at Canberra I realised some of the players had similar problems. I wanted to go to them but knew I wouldn't get the right response by tackling them individually so I spoke to the team about my fears as a player.

We'd been down to Crookwell on a promotional session and were coming back in the night on a small bus. I told them how I'd felt weaker than others but that I walked away not looking down on myself, and when the bus stopped in Canberra there was this eerie silence as they all disappeared into the darkness.

Within 24 hours I had one of the players come to see me personally, and another on the telephone. Both said: "You were talking about *me* last night, weren't you?"

I told them, yes, I had noticed certain things in their games. They just opened up and we talked about fear. Both were high-profile first-graders, and, thankfully, both went on to play a lot more first-grade.

Ever since then I have made a point of openly discussing fear with players.

We had a young fellow here at the Broncos walk and say: "Coach, I get scared out there."

I said: "Sit down, son — this is something I understand . . ."

Fear has nothing to do with size. The little guys weren't hiding behind the door when God handed out courage, and just because a guy's big doesn't necessarily mean he performs as Captain Courageous. Hear the parents on the sidelines at the juniors: "Give it to the big bloke", "Go on, belt him — you're bigger than him."

Somehow, we take the confidence out of these big guys before they even start. It's so important not to question their courage, particularly when they are out there playing the game.

None of us knows how much is inside until faced with an extreme situation, and you're always hearing about and reading wonderful stories about parents saving their children, mates doing extraordinary things for mates.

So in football I have never underrated the value of mateship. See the great teams, it's true, they were great mates. They'd carry an injury for the bloke alongside them, carry on. The sides without mateship are the sides, often, without courage. Mark Twain said courage is the resistance of fear, the mastery of fear, not the absence of fear. And, as usual, he was right.

For myself, as I grow older, I think back to those clubs and players I have known and realise they have helped me to come to grips with my own thoughts on fear. I feel different about it to what I did 20 years ago because, then, I thought I had to have the absence of fear.

I mastered it.

DON'T DROP YOUR BUNDLE, MATE

THIS IS ABOUT MATESHIP.

After a win in August 1995 against Wests, I said the Broncos were playing for each other again. It was an off-the-top-of-the-head statement, something I hadn't thought about, but it had been obvious right through the game it was a fact.

That same week, which coincided with the anniversary of the end of the Pacific War, I got to thinking about mates. What they mean, why mates mean so much.

A mate to me is someone who will not let you down. You trust him, he trusts you and you can both be relied upon.

Recently I read somewhere — and it's right — for the friendship of two, the patience of one is necessary.

Mateship is the reason we do things for one another, in family, in sport and in business. Regardless of how much pay we get, we all need mates; without that common bond we wouldn't achieve nor reach any real heights.

When the Broncos won in '92 and '93 the most dominant factor was mateship.

With your family, mateship can certainly have an impact. More than once my wife is asked the question: who comes first? My mates or her? We've all been asked a similar question, and I just say when asked: "It's a hard question."

When I told her I was going to mention that in this story, she said: "To be honest, Wayne, I'm not that stupid — I don't have to ask."

Around the same time we were beating Wests in '95, I watched a documentary and it had a profound effect on me. It was called *Sandakan*, and was about the atrocities in Borneo during the Second World War: the forced march and the killing of Australian soldiers.

The documentary focused on one of the few remaining soldiers, a good bloke who told how he lost his best mate. They had spent so much time together: firstly in action, then through the prisoner-of-war camps, did the death marches together, and just about made it to the end of the war when his mate was killed. He kept calling him "my mate". He said for the past 45 years he has thought of his mate. Every day.

I once saw a guy named Joe Greene, a Pittsburgh Steelers lineman of the 1970s. He was being interviewed and said there were many times he didn't want to pay the price personally on the football field. He said there's no price he wouldn't pay for his team-mates, however.

There are many times in our lives when we are inclined to let ourselves down but don't, not because of ourselves but because of our mates. In many ways they make us what we are. I've thought about it a lot.

There doesn't have to be danger or adversity around for mateship to shine through. It can be in everyday things, and often, I use these everyday things in talks with the players. Mateship can extend simply to putting yourself out, by putting your mate first. They trudge in from training, thirsty as hell, and the first guy gets to the first cup of water.

You see this guy, knowing how thirsty he is, pick up the cup, turn around and hand it on. He's a mate.

I asked a friend what he thought about mateship and he said it was the thing he'd missed most in the past 10 years. He'd been an underground miner and had had some great mates down there before advancing in the company to a job way above any of that. He now works alone. His mates are still there but he just doesn't see them often.

It's a great loss for sportspeople when they retire, the thing they really miss.

After we'd beaten Wests, I saw my players at the airport really enjoying each other's company. I just stood there thinking that, for a couple of them, it's not all that long before their careers end. I afterwards reminded them of mateship, how it's never to be taken for granted. I showed them this poem; something I first heard when read at the funeral of the father of one of my former players and penned by a good bloke from Roma:

> I've travelled down some lonely roads, both crooked tracks and straight. And I've learnt life's creed. Summed it up in one word: MATE.
> I'm thinking back across the years (a thing I do lately) and these words stick between my ears: "You've got to have a mate."
> My mind goes back to '43, to slavery and hate. When man's one chance to stay alive depended on his mate.
> You'd slip and slither through the mud and curse your rotten fate.
> But then you'd hear a quiet word, "Don't drop your bundle, mate."
> And though it's all so long ago this truth I have to state: a man doesn't know what lonely means till he's lost his mate.
> If there's a life that follows this, if there's a golden gate, the words that I want to hear are just "Good onya mate."
> And when I've left the driver's seat, and handed in the plates, I'll tell old Peter at the door, I've come to join my mates.

Just one last thing: Have you got a mate?

DO YOU RUN OR HIDE?

These two guys are travelling together when they suddenly spy a bear.

Before the bear sees them one man races to a tree, climbs up and hides. The other man isn't so nimble, can't escape and throws himself down and plays "dead".

The bear saunters up and sniffs around. Finally, the bear whispers something into the "dead" man's ear.

Climbing down, the first traveller asks what the bear said. His companion replies: "He told me never to travel with someone who'll desert me at the first sign of danger."

My farmer mate would either lie down beside me or find the strength to carry me high into the tree.

THERE MIGHT BE
NO TOMORROW

WHAT MAKES SPORT AND ITS PEOPLE GREAT IS THAT YOU ARE only ever a game or two away from disaster. Sorry about the lack of romance, but that's a fact. No matter how many great games are behind you, no matter the thickness of your scrapbook, if you don't play well today, there might be no tomorrow.

It's a tough thing for a successful sports person to comprehend, but it is also what allows him to touch on greatness, because he has to keep rising, time and again.

Edwin Moses, the great 400-metre hurdler, was not beaten in a decade. At times he must have had injuries, various excuses, but he kept on rising.

Carl Lewis was the same. Lewis could lose and still be great, still rise. He did this at the 1991 world athletics titles in Tokyo, the first time he was beaten in the long jump. Mike Powell had to break Bob Beamon's world record, set at the 1968 Olympics in Mexico, to outleap Lewis.

So what did Lewis do in the company of this stranger called defeat? He went in the 100 metres and was last of the eight runners at the halfway mark, behind the likes of Fredericks and Burrell and Christie, behind Dennis Mitchell. One by one he pegged them back to win in a world record 9.86 seconds.

Carl Lewis is the kind of guy you want on your team.

Mike Powell? The last time I saw him he had sand in his face in Atlanta, where Lewis won the long jump. Sure, Powell was a gifted athlete, but never one of the greats because he couldn't lift like Lewis.

Greats go that extra notch.

To be in the very top bracket of sport requires tremendous mental application. Being gifted is only the beginning. It's all about priorities.

Like all commitments in life, the priorities need to be in order. Every day of your life.

One of the great decathletes — I think he was American — once revealed how he jumped out of bed every morning and immediately made a list for the day ahead. No 1, every time, was training.

No 2 might have been to pay some bill, or go shopping, and maybe the latest Clint Eastwood movie got a run at No 3.

"Funny thing," added the athlete, "but I never get past the first one."

Routines are at times boring, really boring, and that's where a lot of the guys fall. Regardless of who you are and where you've been, to stay at the top means continuous hard work. You do it for yourself — you have to — but there are some outside responsibilities in delivering the best you possibly can, and they can involve your family or employer.

The delicate balancing comes with another fact of sporting life. You need to be able to enjoy it.

When you're injured, out of form and losing, and the coach tells you to run one more lap or hit one more tackling bag, and you're exhausted . . . there's not a whole lot of enjoyment in that. It comes instead with the camaraderie before, during and after the session or the game.

One afternoon, before an Origin match in 1997, one of the players spoke openly about pressure, how it makes or breaks a player. The players knew that in a few hours not everything would be going to script, but they had to handle that in the right way, not drop their heads, spit the dummy and give up.

The most successful people are the ones who handle adversity in the right manner, and every successful person has confronted adversity.

In modern football, on-field leaders have become even more important, and gone are the days where the one guy, the captain, did all the leading. In that Origin game, Queensland had three designated leaders out there.

It's even tougher on them, but that's life.

CONFIDENCE IS CONTAGIOUS

MANY PEOPLE ARE DEEMED ARROGANT. SOME RIGHTLY, TOO. Away from the sporting fields, look no further than our former political leaders Paul Keating and Wayne Goss.

In my opinion, none of the accused are arrogant people. What I saw in them — and what I see in most successful people — is confidence, just as I see a lack of confidence in those who never achieve their potential.

If you are good at something, anything, you have to be confident in yourself. At times, at the bottom of hills, we see trucks that won't and can't move. They remind me of people without confidence.

Arrogance is an easy thing to label someone with, particularly for those with no comprehension of confidence. To me, arrogance has several meanings, but basically, it's when you're good at what you do and you treat people — friends, workmates, fans — like objects. Like rubbish. They only matter when you're in the mood to give of yourself.

One of the things I've noticed with arrogant people is, when they're down a little on confidence, they need your friendship and support. They need encouragement. But when they're running with the wind: "Hey, what's your name, fella?"

Sure, I know a few football coaches who are arrogant, but I know many more coaches and players who are simply confident. Hard to make the differentiation? No. You just watch the way they treat people, particularly those deemed less important. Even in the team structure.

Muhammad Ali, as was his way, once said: "It's hard to be humble when you're as great as I am." That's probably the height of arrogance. Right? Maybe, but the only place I ever saw the great Ali as being arrogant was in the boxing ring.

At times the Broncos have been described as arrogant. This I know about the Broncos — they're very confident in the way they go about playing football. That's why they and certain other teams, be it in the club, Origin or international arenas, put doubt in their opponents' minds, which is what they set out to do. "Inner arrogance", it's sometimes called.

Certain people are forever confident about their ability, and confidence is contagious, just as the lack of it also rubs off.

The other thing about a confident guy, when he comes off the field he just blends in. With his family, other players suddenly, he's just part. An arrogant guy, he can't do that. Off the field he has to still give a performance when there is no need for one. He has to be on the stage.

All of his sentences begin with "I" and he never has time to listen to anyone.

Joe Garagiola was a Major League catcher and later broadcaster. This is what he had to say: "You're good, you know it. But you don't wear it on your sleeve. You don't have to tell everyone you've got it they already know. If you start telling 'em, it usually ends up lip-service, anyway."

Go Joe.

To be a star, and stay a star, you need a certain air of arrogance about you, confidence, a belief ... body language on the field that says: "I can do this, and you can't stop me."

When the Broncos won back-to-back premierships in 1992–93, Glenn Lazarus used to say: "Let's go out and play with some arrogance." He said it a few times — publicly and privately — and I never felt comfortable with it.

So we sat down and had a talk, and agreed that while the word "arrogance" was being used the meaning had more to do with the confidence we had developed in ourselves and others.

Arrogance can be humiliating in every way. Confidence? It is a glorious celebration of life.

DO SOME PLAYERS HAVE
AN IMAGE PROBLEM?

When I was growing up in rugby league there were a lot of great guys, but the footballer handed the microphone at the function was usually the one who'd had a few too many drinks. His image was not that good and when he'd speak not only would he be embarrassed but also the public.

"Aah," he'd say. "I hate speaking in public."

He'd pause, and add: "Bear with me, aah . . ." Anyway, you know the story.

One of the aspects I'm most proud of in the modern game is the image projected by recently retired players.

I remember an article Ray Price once wrote regarding Bob Lindner, then at Parramatta, whingeing about Bob turning up to training in a BMW.

Price argued rugby league was a working man's game and that its competitors should be seen hurtling down main streets in FJ Holdens, preferably, I suspect, tucking into meat pies at the lights.

At the time I thought what he said and the image he obviously pushed demonstrated a wrong, a lack of imagination. The players of yesterday, you see, if they were seen to be getting ahead, achieving, they were viewed under a different light.

Put simply, they were said to be "up themselves".

Like hell they were.

THE PRICE YOU PAY

TEAMWORK IS A BIT LIKE CONFIDENCE — AT TIMES YOU DON'T know where it comes from; other times, you don't know where it goes.

At finals time, make no mistake, teamwork is the real issue in sport. With so much to win and lose, nothing and no one counts for more.

Like me, you might have wondered why we play football for so long every year, from March through to October. I have finally worked it out this way: our forefathers realised one of the most important ingredients in a season is to allow enough time and training to build a team.

A whole season can give you that opportunity, even though it can take longer. A season allows a team to perform and learn together, to develop trust and confidence in each other and to learn from mistakes made. It creates a culture that allows players' natural talent to come to the forefront.

Where a lot of us have difficulty in becoming part of the team is our own agendas and selfishness. Selflessness is the soul of teamwork.

What teamwork takes is for you to give an enormous amount of yourself.

Then, you have to play your part more times than most, even when you might not like the role you have to play. That's the price, you see, the price you pay to be on a winning team.

Muhammad Ali played his sport as an individual, but spoke for everyone and everything when he said: "Only a man who knows what it's like to be defeated can reach down to the bottom of his soul and come up with the extra ounce of power it takes to win when the match is even."

For a team to develop, you must have great communication.

And honesty is everything.

A lot of us can't handle the truth. We don't like to hear it. Still, all that doesn't mean people have to tell you lies.

Those that can't handle the truth in one big block, you've still got to tell them, but a little bit at a time. The end result's the same.

Mark McCormack, the marketing guru, always worried about people boasting about being always brutally honest. He figured honesty was a good thing, but asked to be left out of the brutality, preferring the little-bit-at-a-time alternative.

It's like when you believe someone likes you, and then another alleged friend jumps up and explains how the other guy, deep down, hates your guts. There's no real need for that, not in one big block.

Communication and honesty should both be aimed at the best possible outcome for the individual and the team.

It's important to keep people informed at all times, whether the news is good or bad.

I like the old adage about communication, and I think it suits, about communicating on a need-to-know basis: If you need to know something, I'll tell you — otherwise, you won't be hearing from me.

Good, no, great teams have trust in each other. It goes back to war and the trenches and the secure feeling of knowing they are there for you and you for them. They have a confidence about themselves that allows you and them to overcome all obstacles in the team's path.

And this confidence in football is never more important than September–October, nearing the end of yet another season.

The key to teamwork, and the Broncos know this, is to work less as individuals and more as a team. And the coach knows not to play his 13 best but his best 13.

At day's end a group working together can accomplish things no individual would dare dream of.

ROLE MODELS

"It's how you play
the game ..."

GET ON THE FRONT FOOT

FOR THE GREAT MAJORITY OF US, PARTICULARLY IN OUR adolescent years, the search is for role models, for appealing qualities and characteristics.

We're all looking for a direction in life, to be better — the smart ones are anyway.

One of the misconceptions about role models is that they have to be football stars, rock singers or politicians, anyone at all with a high profile.

Most of my role models were never superstars at anything, just good people.

There's a responsibility that goes with all of us: it has to do with the way people are always looking at you, watching your every move. And they don't tell you they're looking, they just do it.

At dinner one night I was sitting there with my two daughters. The then 17-year-old said her parents were her role models: and it just reminded me that she's been watching her mum and dad for a long time. Obviously, by her comments, she has been developing her personality based on our actions and behaviour.

My 13-year-old daughter said: "What are role models, Dad?"

I remember watching a movie with the kids when they were a lot younger, a movie called *Pollyanna*, and she was so full of life and fun.

This minister in the movie, he was a pretty negative type of guy. He said: "Until I met you I always looked for the bad in people . . . now you have shown me to look for the good."

It's so important.

We search for role models because very few of us are perfect but we should always look for the good and be smart enough to see the things we don't like and make sure they don't become part of us.

From time to time, I get the odd letter when one of my star players drifts off the track and the general comment is they're not very good role models. To me, though, they're only showing all the imperfections of the rest of us and I think it's a bit sad, because we grab a sports star, put him or her on a pedestal and make out they're some ideal form of human being.

When I picked Gene Miles and, later, Allan Langer to captain the Broncos a major influence was not what they said but what they did.

I want role models to lead our club by their actions, on and off the field.

The thing I know is that every young player coming to our club looks at how the senior players conduct themselves and I know if I have bad role models then I'm going to have a lot of problems with my future stars.

Again, the younger player doesn't just strut up to Allan Langer to tell him: "I'm watching you . . . I admire you."

But he is, and he does. Every move.

The one quality I have always sought in a person is the willingness to stand up for something, just make a stand. Be relied upon, a guy who'll stick in the tough times. Perhaps you will never face tough times together but I still like to have that confidence. No one who doesn't fit that bill has ever had any influence on my life.

Take my uncle, Eddie Brosnan. He played football, played for Australia. He was at this function, and he didn't mind a drink, Eddie, a very tough man.

Eddie wasn't in this argument but his friend was. Eddie walked over and said to this other guy: "If you want to take on my friend, you have to take me on too."

The guy said it had nothing to do with Eddie, who shook his head: "It has everything to do with me. He is my friend. If he's wrong, I'm wrong."

Eddie Brosnan was like that all of his life, so rock solid. I remember one night I was in a car, saw his, and followed it. He thought I was the police, so he stopped and I stopped behind him, thinking he wanted to talk to me. He wanted to talk all right, even though he didn't know it was me.

He stormed up to challenge what he thought was the police following him.

"Oh it's you, boy," he said. "I was going to go on the front foot."

It wasn't that he didn't respect the police — he was a policeman himself — it's just that he challenged situations he saw as wrong.

It's a characteristic I've always looked for. You have a lot of great mates but they're not necessarily role models. The problem is, whether it's dance or gymnastics, football or politics, many people find their role model and become totally obsessed with them when they should not be so narrow-minded and instead look at other people and other walks of life. We must always remain ourselves.

Sure, take a little piece here, a little bit there, and blend them into your own personality but never too many bits, not so that you become a false commodity. Someone else.

I was very much influenced by our military history, particularly as a kid. Just reading. Lining up down the main street on Anzac Day had a powerful effect on me.

I'd ask myself if I had been born in a different era, how would I have handled war? These men, they were no different from us. They questioned themselves, too, it's just that they had no choice but to find the answers.

Anzac Day, to me, glorifies nothing. It's just a reminder, an insight.

Growing up, whenever I was asked to do something hard, mostly physically but sometimes mentally, and I felt exhausted, that I just couldn't do it, I'd think of the soldiers, their hardships.

Somehow, it gave me strength, the strength not to give up. As you read this story you might ask yourself one question. A simple question. What type of role model are you?

A FEW GOOD, HONEST, INFLUENTIAL MEN

OFTEN I'M ASKED ABOUT THE PEOPLE TO HAVE MOST INFLUENCED my coaching. Apart from my own experiences as a player, the most influence has come from three guys who became great mates of mine.

The first was Bob Bax, a very successful coach in Queensland and a very good friend.

Then there was Jack Gibson.

I was a coach a long time before I first met big Jack. I just admired what he did for rugby league, how he did it and the things he preached. Today, I think of Jack as probably having had the biggest influence on what I am as a coach.

There is no doubt he was the most influential coach in our game and possibly in all the team games in our country. Jack made everyone realise the importance of the coach. Until Jack Gibson, coaches were second-class citizens. All the recognition went to the players and officials and, while I wouldn't mind if that still happened, Jack somehow made the coach a part of the team.

Before Jack — and the old fellas will tell you this — the coach just had to make sure the balls were pumped up for training.

"Hey guys, who we playin' today?"

"Wests."

"Hah, see ya at 'alf time — we'll kick those guys' butts."

Jack Gibson changed all that, and I'm a full-time coach today through him in more ways than one. He was the first full-time coach; now there's not a part-timer. The conditions and benefits we in the game enjoy today, and the way we play today, are courtesy of the Jack Gibson era.

And it was Jack who gave us the great team concepts, introducing the coordinator (Ron Massey), the fitness guy (Mick Souter) and the sports-medicine guy (Alf Richards) when sports medicine was in its infancy.

The first to concentrate on weight-training, so significant in the modern game. Pre-season camps, motivational films ... in '74, when Paul Broughton was coaching us at Brothers, he got this film called *The Second Effort*. I remember Paul saying, "This comes from Jack Gibson."

It was about Vince Lombardi and a salesman, and to this day it is the best film I have seen.

Jack found it in America and I've heard some of his friends say he thinks of himself as a reborn American, with those one-liners and such.

That's another thing, the video — Jack introduced the video to rugby league and it has had a greater impact on our game than just about anything or anyone.

The video made us all better coaches. Jack, he kicked off with black-and-white film, recording players' mistakes. In the old days, when we threw a bad pass we all had such a bad memory that when the coach brought it up on Tuesday night you couldn't remember it happening, and, basically, it was his word against yours.

Jack could prove it in black-and-white and, together, you could fix it.

It was Jack who formed the players' association, because he always believed in the players having a voice and respectability in the game. Discipline, he gave us that too, convincing his players there was no room for cheap shots.

Black-tie dinners for players, tackle counts . . . there's a good yarn. Harry Bath was quite a successful coach himself and when Jack introduced tackle counts, old Harry said he had no use for them, that he could tell how a player was tackling without keeping count. Some time later, Harry replaced a prominent player mid-match and back in the rooms, when asked why by a journo, replied: "His tackle count was too low."

Jack got rid of selectors. Once I heard him asked what he thought of selectors? "Aren't they tiny things in the gearbox of a car?"

In his early coaching days even Jack had to put up with selectors and at St George, they tell me, they'd get to Graeme Langlands and the selectors obviously would want Langlands in the team but Jack would fight against it. Finally, he'd give in, and they'd move on to another established international and again he'd fight it. Then it would happen: Jack would want some unknown kid in the team and he'd say, "Come on fellas, I gave you Langlands and Smith, ya gotta give me one back."

They labelled him, unfairly, a defensive coach but I doubt Jack ever told Russell Fairfax, Mark Harris, Ian Schubert, Steve Ella, Eric Grothe, Arthur Beetson or Brett Kenny not to run.

He taught us that winners didn't just hang around the sideline waiting for the ball and of tackling drills previously unknown. When they brought him up to coach Queensland Country I remember one of our greatest coaches, Duncan Thompson, just before his death, watching these tackling drills.

Old Duncan walked over and shook Jack by the hand, saying: "I'm very impressed — in all my years I have never seen players being coached in defence."

This week, every kid in every park training to play rugby league was touched, in some way, by Jack Gibson.

Even before I began coaching I used to love watching him on TV. I just used to laugh and laugh. I loved the way he handled reporters, and the way he made nothing sound really something.

He has this presence that makes you sense he wouldn't fail you and you wouldn't want to fail him. You want to please him because you know he's not lying to you, not trying to con you.

Jack figured coaching was done through the week, and if he had nothing to say just before the match or at halftime, he said nothing. The only halftime speech he ever remembered as a player was when it was pouring rain, mud everywhere, from the field to the dressing rooms, and this coach, dressed in a beautiful suit and totally upset with his players' tackling, dived bang into the mud, screaming: "This is the way you tackle."

I like what he stands for, the honesty bit and the team, the way he does things for people who can do nothing for him. I liked his coaching — and I love the man. He stood up for people and the game and he coached players not only in football but in life. In the process he produced some great football teams and some greater human beings.

The two characteristics great leaders must have is respect and a presence. Jack had those two, no worries.

He wrote a number of books and he's presently writing another, but I particularly love the foreword by Singo in *When All is Said and Done*. It's a wonderful foreword.

"I don't know about you," wrote Singo, "but I'm sick of success seminars conducted by failures. I am tired of clichéd motivational speakers and goal-setters. But I never tire of the lessons of life learnt from games won and lost."

That's exactly what Jack is — a lesson of life.

I suppose Jack sees things in people they don't always see in themselves. He's the reason I'm Broncos coach. When the owners were granted their licence in 1987, one of their first ports of call was Jack Gibson, for advice on who should be the coach.

Jack apparently said there was only one guy for the job, a young guy at Canberra working with Don Furner. The directors soon came knocking.

One of my great regrets is that I wish I could have played under him, because I know I would have played for him. That's the greatest accolade a player can give a coach. It's not "thanks" or "I appreciated that"; it's that he played for him. Tried for him.

Behind every great man they say there's a great woman and I'm sure Judy Gibson is such a person, but there is another person who has been standing behind Jack since the very first day he coached — the third person to have had a great influence on my coaching: Ron Massey.

I met Ron long after I met Jack. It was 1987 and we, as in the Raiders, had just played Cronulla, where Jack was coaching.

As much as I was in awe of Jack's persona, I was as much in awe of Ron because he was always prepared to be the silent partner. He has this presence and strength of character, things you don't always sense or see in people straight up.

Over the years I have relied on Ron for advice and direction.

And Ron, without knowing it, has influenced me in many things. But his greatest influence on me has been his honesty. With friends, you can tell them that you're not always happy with them, when they're wrong, and still be their friends.

I don't know of any other person I've ever met who has such a strong sense of duty and rightness. He's hard to win an argument with — in fact he impossible, even when he's wrong.

Recently, Ron's been very sick. The year 2001 . . . it was a very tough year for me because a number of my friends and their families got hurt. Bob Bax had just died and Paul Morgan, a wonderful friend and mentor, died on Australia Day. Then down went Ron with his severe illness.

For a long time we didn't talk about what we needed to talk about.

One of the great friendships is Ron and Jack's, and when Ron was extremely sick and allowed no visitors except family, we heard all about the day Jack walked down the hospital corridor.

"Family only, Mr Gibson," said the nurse.

"I am family," said Jack, growling. And continuing.

When I was thinking about making a career of coaching I studied Jack Gibson and noticed that he never stayed at the one club for a long time. Intrigued, I asked Ron about this fact many years later, about why Jack always seemed to leave after only three or so seasons.

Ron explained that it took Jack only three years to get all the officials offside, that he upset them something terrible.

Jack loved coaching NSW in Origin. I wasn't coaching Queensland one year so he felt safe in ringing and asking about a player I'd had something to do with.

"Wayne, what do you think of that boy Coyne?"

"Gary Coyne, playing at Canberra?"

"Yeah, that boy Coyne. I'm thinking about putting him in the team."

"What team?"

"New South Wales."

"Well, that's a good idea, Jack — except he's a Queenslander."

"I obviously can't have him then, Wayne, can I? Hope your mob don't realise he can play."

I just love talking to him, listening and learning. Jack and Eric Cox and Ray Warren organised a testimonial lunch for Ron and so many great people turned up and listened and clapped and enjoyed one another's company. There were some great players there, and I remember looking at the players and looking at Ron and Jack and marvelling at what it would have been like to be part of their era, their time. Ray Price and Mick "The Crow" Cronin, Peter Sterling and Brett Kenny, Steve Edge, Peter Wynn, Bob "The Bear" O'Reilly and Gavin Miller.

Ron was not completely over his illness but was, as usual, looking for someone to gee up when a couple of the boys behind the microphone told the great "watch" yarn.

We're going back quite a few years here, but the yarn stands as one of rugby league's greats.

It centres around Parramatta and the mighty prop Bear O'Reilly.

Anyway, The Bear's upset this time because the committee and the players simply don't appreciate all that he offers the club, and they never give him anything or say anything and, well, The Bear's always complaining about it.

So Ron is walking through a fair down Pitt Street in the city when he spies this shiny, whacking big gold watch for sale at the princely sum of $4.50. It's got a fancy French name on it, too, except it's spelt a little wrong but this is evident to few, and definitely not to growling big bears.

Now it's Saturday morning training at Cumberland Oval, the day before a vital match against Manly. And Ron has organised a special presentation, to be made by Mick Cronin.

The players circle The Crow as the champion centre calls The Bear out of the pack for a special award, a vote of thanks and admiration from his humble peers.

Well, after receiving the most impressive looking timepiece, The Bear is close to tears, mumbling how the players appreciate him even if the committee doesn't. One after one the players walk over to have a good look at the gold watch until The Bear becomes a trifle suspicious. Finally, he roars: "Is there something wrong with this watch?"

Ron Massey grabs the watch, sings out, "You dirty ungrateful bastard", throws it on the ground and stomps on it before tearing off in seeming disgust.

The Bear is most upset, down on all fours trying to pick up the pieces but with no hope of putting it together again. The players are saying how poor old Ron had gone around them raising the money, how he'd gone into the city to buy the best.

The Bear, he was close to tears. Later in the day Mick Cronin call Ron with fears The Bear would not be able to play against Manly, such was his distress. So Ron relented and allowed The Crow to call the Bear and expose the joke.

Parramatta won.

Never underrate the power of team spirit and the role of the gee-up in it. Jack was always the straight guy, Ron the joker, yet so ethical and strong of character. And *honest*.

At day's end, these two guys didn't need another 13 people to be a team.

NOTHING BEATS
THE REAL THING

We were at South Brisbane in the late winter of '79, a week short of playing the preliminary final, when Souths Juniors' president Jack Astill strutted up. "Can I do anything for you?" said Jack.

I nodded, explaining that, yeah, there was one thing — I'd love to have Jack Gibson spend a day with our players.

When Jack Gibson walked into Brothers that week I was like a kid in a toyshop.

For so long I'd studied this great coach from afar, and, suddenly, here he was in person, with such wonderful humility and knowledge of life.

After just one working day he made you feel as if you had known him all your life, that you could trust him and that he trusted you.

He was leaving, and I said: "Jack, if we win on Sunday I've got this film to show them next week."

Dry as you like, he turned and replied: "When I'm gone, Wayne, ya gunna need somethin' special."

And he was right.

We won the preliminary final but got belted the next week in the grand final. The film, obviously, was not special enough — what we really needed was another day with Jack Gibson.

A PROUD AND EMOTIONAL MAN

SOME PEOPLE GET EXCITED DRIVING TO THE GOLD COAST, TO Movie World or to the beach, but back in 1984 the most exciting trip a Brisbane football coach could make was in the other direction, over to the playing fields of downtown Ipswich.

There a little fellow called Kevin Walters was just beginning to live out his big dreams, throwing footballs between his legs and around his back, charging to support his twin brother, Kerrod, like there was no tomorrow, and generally mesmerising the opposition.

You talk about exciting.

Sure, they had bad habits and, equally sure, a lot to learn, which was soon emphasised when the brothers Walters arrived late for their first training session with the Queensland Under 18s.

They smiled, then frowned, blaming the train, an old red rattler, and I remember giving them a serve.

When I went south to coach Canberra in 1987 I took with me two guys: Peter Jackson and Kevin Walters. Kevvie had played Under 19s at Ipswich as well as some first grade, but he was ready and I took him.

Just a year later the Broncos were forming and I didn't want to go home without him. He still had two years to go on his contract and when I went to say I was sorry to be leaving he said not to worry, that he was happy in Canberra.

In 1990, his contract up, St George offered him $75,000 and the Broncos offered him $25,000 — Kevin Walters came home.

I know a little bit about the guy: have seen him grow up, win five premierships with the Broncos, been to his 21st, his engagement, his wedding, the christening of his three sons, and to the funeral of his wife.

He represents everything you could want in a person, and in a friend. He is fun. Loyal. He speaks his mind. And he will never, ever let you down.

Often in life you hear people talking about "family men". Talk's cheap. Kevin Walters is a family man. Today take one look at those three boys and the commitment he has made to them.

His parents, Sandy and Kevin (KG), you just don't meet better people. You can see their character and their traits in all of the sons, but particularly Kevvie, who looks more like KG than KG himself.

People also talk about his great combination with Allan Langer, a combination borne out of friendship. In a decade playing together they were partners in performance, and partners in mateship. Kevvie was a great foil for Alf, because he could read what Alf was going to do. If Alf was the heart and soul of the Broncos, Kevvie has been our emotion, a side to the guy that I love. He needs you to believe in him. And I do.

Back a couple of seasons now, he had a real thing about quitting the Broncos and moving to Townsville to play with the Cowboys. During it all, I went around and saw Kim, who, at that stage, didn't know whether or not she was going to get through her battle with breast cancer. Kim opened the door, and smiled. "Kim, he doesn't understand," I said. "The worst thing that can happen to you and to him now is to leave here, leave the support." Kim said she appreciated that, and knew it was right. Kevvie? He never knew about the visit.

Going into that 1997 season, we were off to Papua New Guinea for a trial match, and the night before Kevvie, all fired up, rang to say he wasn't going to New Guinea, that he wasn't doing this and he wasn't doing that and the Broncos could, well, take a hike.

The following morning I got to the airport early and found the seat where I could best look down the corridor at the passengers flowing in. I had never sat and looked down a corridor before, and I seemed to be doing it for a very long time.

All of a sudden in he walked. We won the Super League premiership that year, and the NRL premiership the following year, with Kevvie leading the way and finally playing for Australia.

He set up the Kim Walters Choices Program with the drive and commitment we have come to expect. The emotion, too. In 16 years I have seen this young man go through everything, and come out the same.

Never have I felt more proud of a guy than when Kevin Walters led Queensland out of the tunnel in front of 90,000-odd screaming fans at Stadium Australia for the second game of the 1999 Origin series. Pride and emotion. It was the highlight — the salute — to everything he has done. To everything we have done together.

A DREAMER WHO SAW THINGS
WE CANNOT IMAGINE

HOW DO YOU TELL AUSTRALIAN PIONEERS? BY THE KNIVES IN their backs, that's how.

I used this line to farewell Paul Morgan when he retired as chairman of the Broncos. Paul Morgan, for the uninitiated, was one of Australia's great characters. A pioneer.

Though friends for 25 years since playing for the All Whites in Toowoomba as young men, we remained throughout his life chalk and cheese.

He was Porky and I'm thin. He had a sense of humour and I don't. He was loud and I mumble. He was an open communicator, holding nothing back, and I communicate on a need-to-know basis. He was a chain-smoker and I chew mints. He laughs.

Sure, we were both into fitness . . . but I wouldn't want an introduction to his trainer.

What we shared was a common love of people, extending to those in sport with only limited ability being given every opportunity. Through sport, it is important to create an environment for young people to grow into adults.

He was a dreamer, a great dreamer, and dreams are wiser than scientific formulas or anything a mathematician can whip up. Dreamers see things we cannot imagine and, if we're lucky, they share them with us.

Another thing, he was a great Queenslander and only Queenslanders know what makes a great Queenslander. When the Broncos were born he wanted them to be *Queensland's* team, for everyone in the State to feel proud.

This pride, this patriotism, extends to business. I know Paul Morgan had countless opportunities to set up his stockbroking business in Sydney, but he stayed in Brisbane to build Paul Morgan Securities.

Simply because of his belief in Queensland. The guys he went to uni with, they're in Sydney.

Poor souls.

The yarns about him are many, but I would like to share just a couple, at the same time burying a fallacy.

Come back to the first Origin game of 1987, when Queensland were beaten on the hooter by NSW. According to sporting lore, I was so shattered that I walked the streets of Brisbane until three in the morning, in a blubbering, blundering state.

Part of this is true — the shattered part — but the rest has to do with Paul Morgan.

I was walking out of Lang Park, kicking cans and looking for dogs, when he charged up in his big, black car, wound down the window and barked: "I want to talk to you."

For the next three or four hours he listed reasons why I should become Broncos coach and I remember when he subsequently came to Canberra, where I was coaching, how he wouldn't leave my favourite lounge chair until I had agreed. Hours and hours.

The move from Lang Park to ANZ Stadium is the gutsiest thing I ever saw done by him and the Broncos board.

To know him was to know generosity, how he helped those who couldn't help him — and that is, after all, how you judge character. If there was a battler around wanting to get to the top, Paul Morgan was never far away.

With the players at the Broncos, his priority was to see them successful after football. He genuinely cared about them and their futures.

At the close of the 1995 season, realising things would change at our club with a company known as Pacific Sports Entertainment taking over, I wrote him a letter. I don't write many letters, but I just wanted to thank him.

For the opportunities.

For his confidence in me, his generosity.

I wish for his gift to treat the common man and the leader of the nation just the same.

For, at day's end, it's not the critic who counts but the man in the street whose space is marred by blood and sweat.

Over the years, people at the Broncos will forget Paul Morgan. But not while I'm around.

You could never protect him because he has this great ability to inflict pain upon himself. I accepted him for the man he is — you knock him down, and he got straight back up on you.

Paul Morgan was the man in the arena. He erred and he triumphed and, finally, spent himself on a worthy cause.

You see, Porky died suddenly, in January 2001, on Australia Day. This was my eulogy . . .

Paul Morgan — where do you start? To say "larger than life" is a cliché, but those of us whose lives he touched were dwarfed by his caring, his generosity, his honesty, his time for you and his fierce loyalty to family and friends and anything Queensland.

I first met him in 1970 in Toowoomba. Me a young policeman, and Paul working for a fertiliser company. We were both playing for All Whites. That was the last year Toowoomba won the Bulimba Cup against Brisbane. Paul was in the team and I was on the bench. We became friends very quickly. I would call and see him at work and he would tell me his dreams. I have never seen anybody physically push themselves harder than Paul at training and most nights he would vomit towards the end of the session. He left Toowoomba just after the Bulimba Cup win to return to Brisbane and play for Redcliffe.

I got into coaching and he got into business and started to fulfil his dreams. I would read about him in the Business Section and he would sometimes catch my name in the Sports Section. (Usually in an article about my inability as a coach.)

Then 1987 was upon us quickly and someone mentioned that Brisbane were to be admitted to the NSW Rugby League and in charged Paul with his partners, Steve Williams, Barry Maranta and Gary Balkim to form the Broncos. I was all settled in Canberra when the larger-than-life figure of Paul Morgan arrived at my home at 8.30am with my accountant in tow. I answered the front door and there's Paul holding this big port. I asked what he was doing and what was the port for. "You keep rejecting my offers to coach the Broncos," he said. "I am staying at your home until you say 'yes'." Four hours later, with a headache, I went for a run by myself and decided that I would take the job. I have said it before: Paul Morgan was the only person who could have convinced me to break a contract. I still regret that to this day, however I don't regret the next 13 years I was to spend with Paul and the Broncos.

So what did I learn in those 13 years with this character who wore his heart on his sleeve, who could be intimidating, who could get cranky and say things that would hurt but for whatever human weaknesses you would forgive immediately and try and do your absolute best for him because you knew he would not let you down and you did not want to let him down. Why? Because he was your mate, that's why.

He was a leader amongst leaders. School Captain at State High, and regarded as their best ever School Captain. Kids from grade 8 to grade 12 thought the world of him, and still do. Great leaders make decisions and very rarely change them. That was Paul. Leaders don't blink. I saw him in a lot of tight situations and a couple involved me. He never hesitated. He knew what had to be done and he did it. Leaders also know that only time will vindicate their decisions. At times you can't justify, or explain why you do things and sometimes you know that only time will prove you right. Paul got a lot right.

Paul was also a great dreamer and unlike most people who dream all night, wake up and trudge off into another day of drudgery — Paul would bounce out of bed after a few hours sleep (too busy dreaming) to toddle (barge) off to turn his dreams into reality. He dreamt of the Broncos being the best and made the statement after our first premiership — "This is the start of the Broncos Dynasty." I nearly choked him for that. He just replied "You don't whack it up 'em enough, Wayne!" He dreamed of Paul Hogan wrestling fake crocs, all the way to Hollywood. He dreamed about Morgan Stockbroking being a leading company in this State, while at the time he had employed only two people. Morgan Stockbroking became a national company.

Most of all, however, he dreamed of success for others — usually Queenslanders, many of whom he barely knew. He loved this State but most of all he loved the people that make it what it is, and wanted them to dream and become better too.

He hated seeing young talent wasted and he was always on my number about the young Broncos and what they were achieving away from football. We shared that bond.

All good people have skill, dedication and ability. Paul had a little extra — he had determination. And that is what made the difference for him.

Over the years, Paul gave away bikes to tri-athletes, bought rowing eights and fours for State High. The school wanted to dedicate these to Paul, but he would have none of that and told them to dedicate the eight to his former Principal, George Lockie. Paul was a very generous and humble man. I hated his knockers because they sought perfection from him, whilst being imperfect themselves. It was his imperfections that I loved most *about him because I saw how much he gave, asking for nothing in return. In my eyes this is what character is. It has been said that a man's character can be judged by what he does for those who can do nothing for him, which makes Paul "Porky" Morgan one of the great characters of our time.*

GREAT QUARTERBACK, GREAT JUDGE

I once spent a week with the Denver Broncos in the NFL, with the great John Elway. Those quarterbacks, they're treated like gods, the way everybody talks about them, the staff, the other players, the kids with the autograph books.

Elway's a big fellow, a lovely guy, too. We had a couple of conversations and I watched him train. He must be at least 6ft 2in (188cm), Elway, and the way he moved, you'd probably play him at lock instead of halfback.

Quarterbacks, they need a great throwing arm, and again like halfbacks, great vision. When to pass, when to hold, what option to take. I remember showing Denver a video of our Broncos playing, and apart from getting excited about the lack of padding and the body contact, one player caught their attention. After just a few minutes, I think it was Elway who said: "That guy the No. 6, he's pretty smart, isn't he? Looks like he really controls the game for you."

The No. 6 was Wally Lewis.

THE SHARK WHO WANTED
IT SO MUCH

ROCKET SCIENTISTS HAD AN OPINION ABOUT IT. AND GARBOS. Train drivers and neurosurgeons, footballers and fans. Sheikhs and sheilas. From the back o' Bourke to Bosnia, in April 1996 just about everyone got their tongues around Greg Norman and the US Masters.

As a race, we are so influenced by what we read and hear, and it was more than interesting to watch the reaction to Norman's defeat in Augusta.

The world media could easily have savaged him. Had that been the case, much of the comment in streets and bars and homes would have been a lot more negative. So the media, for one, gets a big tick.

Norman, he gets a bigger tick. Regardless of what happened in that Masters, Greg Norman, to me, is a winner and has always been a winner.

We love our sports stars to win, but no matter how many tournaments Greg Norman wins over the years, I believe history should record his triumph as the way he handled himself in defeat in the US Masters of 1996.

As American football coach Bear Bryant once said, "When you make a mistake there are only three things you should ever do about it: admit it; learn from it; and, three, don't repeat it."

There's no doubting that individual sports are much harder than team sports because individuals can't hide behind anything or anyone. Too often when we make mistakes we attribute fault to everyone bar ourselves.

If Greg Norman gave us nothing else in his wonderful career, he certainly gave us the strength and courage to say, hey, I goofed it. I made a mistake.

Contrary to what some believe and feel, there is no more famous Australian, no other Australian who commands such an audience.

My players at the Broncos talked about him at different stages through the week after that Masters. They reckon the first time Greg Norman double-bogeyed he knew that the world knew he was gone, that he would have felt like crawling into the first hole he found and disappearing. Disappearing to his house with a click of the fingers, bypassing the media and the galleries, everyone.

But he knew he couldn't take that road. So he confronted it. He handled it. In the best possible way.

Sure I have heard people, both publicly and privately, say he choked. I absolutely hate that word, that terminology, and it is a reference I never use in coaching.

For the majority of us to succeed at something it is a learned experience. That's why you always hear people talking about the 100-game first-grade player, or the 10-year veteran, because they have learned.

Greg Norman is no different to many of us. He just wanted it so much and, at times, when you want something so much it can turn everything around and become your enemy.

Take rugby league. It's halftime, and you're leading well. It's a big game, a tough game. So you go out in the second half intent on not making any mistakes instead of doing what you did in the first half, and that is playing flat out. What happens? You lose, that's what. It just happens.

Self-doubt is not all wrong. Self-doubt, again at times, gives you the strength to go on. John Madden, another American football coach, said: "Once something is done there are two things you have to do — evaluate what happened, and work towards it not happening again."

I have no doubt that by the time of his post-tournament press conference Greg Norman had evaluated what had happened and was already working towards it not happening again.

After the third day of play, the commentators were quite excited about Nick Faldo's round, meaning he would play alongside Norman on the final day. The great thing about Greg Norman is that Faldo knew Norman was going to bring out the best in him, but he could not have known the extent of the best. Faldo did not only play brilliantly, but acted brilliantly in victory. Once, you might remember, they called him Nick-the-you-know-what. Faldo is down as telling the press, "I want to thank you from the heart of my bottom." But at Augusta, Norman brought out the best in Faldo in every way, the main one being humility . . . humanity. Somehow, Greg Norman made Faldo Nick-the-Nice.

Tom Watson missed the cut this time around, a rarity, but his words were still there on the last two days and, indeed, forever. "Sometimes," said Watson, "you have to lose majors before you can win them. It's the price you pay for maturing. The more times you can put yourself into pressure situations, the more times you compete, the better off you are. It's a learning experience that's worth a fortune."

Some of us have to take more knocks than others. I don't know why, why some seem to have all the luck. The opportunities.

When we look back over Greg Norman's career, over the majors and the way he kept coming back, and someone asks what made him so great, you just tell them: "Every time he fell over, he got up again."

ALF

I KNOW ALLAN LANGER TO BE A REMARKABLE CHARACTER IN every way, but I still have to question his remarks explaining away his longevity when he reached the 200-game mark for the Broncos in 1997.

"A great trainer and stretcher," he said.

All right, now for the truth!

Pound-for-pound, as they say in boxing, he was rugby league's top performer of the 1990s. Day in, day out. Year after year. By "performer", I'm not just talking natural gifts. He has those, but what he also has is a determination and dedication to always put in.

I once heard Peter Sterling summarising Alf's career, saying how he knew from the first time he set eyes on him in Origin 1987 he was going to be a star. To Sterling, and to a lot of us, the most important thing is that Alf is still the same bloke who ran out that night, unaffected by it all.

Cyril Connell, our talent scout at the Broncos, played halfback for Australia in the 1950s and he has repeatedly told me he's never seen a better No. 7 than Alf.

We have had so many great halfbacks: some had great kicking games, some brilliant speed and others were simply tough and ultra competitive. Alf was and remains the entire package.

Some things about him stand out to me. I have to say he has certainly helped my career as a coach. Apart from Tommy Raudonikis, I'm the only person in Australia to have coached him in A-grade. In the beginning he wasn't a good defensive player, but he taught himself how to tackle, to the point that every Sunday we marvelled at and relied on his defence. It's true, the leg did help him a bit, but because of his so-called "style" they changed the rules of the game and everything was forgiven.

There's another thing he never had in the beginning — a long kicking game. He always had a short kicking game but when he joined the Broncos, Wally Lewis was the dominant player and the dominant kicker.

After Wally, Alf taught himself a long kicking game. Like tackling, it wasn't natural for him, but it became so. And that's what I admire about him. He doesn't rely on God-given gifts.

I have to tell you about his most embarrassing moment because he certainly won't. It happened when the Queensland Super League team was in New Zealand for a Tri-Series match.

We were having a drink — a light drink — and he was at this fun machine thing, you know, with the puck and the wooden players on those turning rods, when the puck got caught and he cut his thumb trying to dislodge it.

It looked to be only a small cut but it started to bleed and I said he'd better go and get some tissues or something. A few minutes passed and I'm looking at him, and I start to see him go very pale. He starts to stagger backwards. I grab him as he falls to the floor.

"You OK?"

"Not really," he says.

As he's staggering backwards, I put my arm around him. He's limp and, suddenly, flat on the floor. He's fainted at the sight of his own blood, so we take him outside the club.

When he came to, we couldn't help but laugh at the master of the gee-up, who, this time, was very embarrassed.

He said: "Coach, how about going down there and telling them I've been rushed off to hospital for microsurgery? Ask them to stop drinking and go to bed as a mark of respect for me. If you don't, they're really going to give it to me in the morning."

I obliged, but the boys refused to budge, and after a good while Alf reappeared, his hand heavily bandaged, and said: "Don't worry, fellas, the microsurgeon has been able to stitch the thumb back on."

We call him "The Money Man" at the Broncos because we know that when he's on his game, everybody is in for a winning day. He carries the tag and responsibility extremely well and I think he only ever questioned it once.

"Do I have to play well for us to win?" he asked. I explained, the best way I could, that because he was such a linchpin, so dominant, when he was off his game it was simply different. No, he didn't have to play well for us to win. We do win without him, as the records show, but it always helps to have him.

ALF AND THE GG

My farmer mate Ged has a young bull, as farmers tend to do. He calls it GG, something to do with it being a pretty tough-looking character. He's only a little bull, GG, and when he got among the heifers quite a few months back it apparently wasn't a pretty sight.

Anyway, his first calf was born. Born really small, too, and after calving problems that you and I, according to my farmer mate, wouldn't believe. But the calf quickly bounced up and began darting here and there around the paddock.

Little but tough. So he called it "Alf".

I laughed, and said: "You got the name right."

FAIRYTALES CAN COME TRUE

UNBELIEVABLE, IT WAS, SO STUPEFYINGLY UNBELIEVABLE. OF THE five magnificent State of Origin series I'd been involved in, there's no doubt that 2001 *was* and *is* and forever *will be* the most special.

The reasons are many. Initially, the selfish part of me wanted little to do with the coaching job. But the Queensland part of me realised that as a State and a team and as individuals we just couldn't contend with another 2000, when New South Wales won the third game so decisively.

So, with a lot of issues, I accepted the job. With a lot of doubt, I guess, wondering how quickly we, as in Queensland, could rebuild. What might the scoreboards show? What if we didn't manage to win a game?

I put all that aside, as I had put it aside in the past, basically because I had no control over any of those things.

The real question was: what *could* we control?

Game I in Brisbane provided a great start. The Blues were complacent on the night — a night I felt to be, with the exception of the first ever game exactly 20 years earlier, the most crucial in Queensland's Origin history.

But sadly for Queensland, Game II came around without Gorden Tallis, our inspiration.

NSW had been hurt by the first loss, and this time they played superbly. We were close — very close — to getting heavily beaten, but in the end it was just a beating. That was the most important thing, not to be heavily beaten, as it would have destroyed our confidence.

After the game a friend saw me holed up with a selector in a quiet corner of the change room, and weeks later, when he read that Alf was coming back to play for Queensland, he boasted that he had witnessed, then and there, the hatching of the plan.

He was right to a degree, as it was in that dressing room after that game that we realised that, as things stood, Queensland couldn't win Game III. What would the score be with no Tallis and his inspiration, with so many fine players out injured?

Sure, we were still at one-all, and that was a great effort, but I left the Olympic Stadium knowing we had to do something different.

Back at the hotel I grabbed four guys, and said: "You've all played for Australia, and you've played for Queensland — now sit down and name for me the two most inspirational players you have come across?"

Kevin Walters got a couple of votes, as did Gorden Tallis, but all four named Allan Langer.

This was exactly what I wanted to hear, reinforcing my thoughts on what Alf meant to teams and individuals. I didn't know how he'd perform in Game III but I did know the value of his presence and how that presence alone would give us belief.

But to be truthful, even this wasn't the beginning of the plan. After Origin I, who should I have run into but the former Broncos and Queensland prop Andrew Gee. He was back from England having an old injury treated. It was late, a long night, and all I wanted to ask him about was Alf. Andrew said Alf was in great form over there, that he'd never seen him train harder. Me, I said nothing to no one.

One month, a defeat and a five-man meeting later, I left Sydney for Brisbane on a mission: Warrington, Alf's club side in England, had to say OK; I had to convince officials on both sides of the border; and I had to convince the Queensland selectors. I didn't care what anyone else thought.

So I got home and made a phone call.

"Alf, how would you feel about coming home to play for Queensland?"

"What's taken you so long to ask, coach?"

"Do you think you're up to it?"

"Do you really think I'd come home and embarrass myself?"

He's a champion, Alf, because that's always been his motivation — the smallest guy but the best player, year in year out.

That's why he retired when he did. At the Broncos in 1999 we'd won one of 10 games. Others would make excuses. Not Alf.

He wouldn't play with guys who weren't putting in, with guys who were embarrassing themselves. He'd say, "Coach, get him out of the team."

So when he said, "Do you really think I'd come home and embarrass myself", well, that's all I wanted to hear.

Alf was genuinely waiting for that call. Every night when he went to bed he said it was his wish to play again for Queensland or the Broncos.

Gene Miles was the first selector I approached. You should have seen the look. "Geno," I said, "I'm not on anything and I haven't lost the plot — but we should bring Alf home for Game III."

Well . . .

Geno said: "Whatttttt????????"

I said we weren't even going to discuss it straight away. I asked him to go away and think it through for 20 minutes.

About half an hour went by, and Geno rang to say he thought it was a great idea.

One of the Queensland officials proved a bit of an obstacle, but he came over, and NSW, to their credit, seemed to see the sense in it pretty much straight off.

Before the 2001 series even kicked off, in the back of my mind I'd wondered whether we'd need one of the overseas-based Queenslanders. So Ross Livermore, the QRL boss, had run it by his NSW counterparts and they'd agreed then that they'd consider it.

Warrington, they were great, and by the Wednesday everything was passed and ticked by everyone. It's not easy keeping these things in-house, and it must rate as one of the great coups keeping this secret until the day Alf was actually named publicly in the Queensland squad.

Psychologically, it had to give us some sort of advantage. Say NSW knew earlier, maybe they would have picked someone else in their squad, maybe not. Just little things, adding up, all to your advantage. It's announced, and it's a surprise.

Alf arrives, and holds centre stage for the next eight days. There is no other sports story in Australia. And everybody has a theory about it.

I knew Alf was fit and playing OK, and I didn't care about the theories.

He arrived on the Sunday night and when we went into camp on the Monday I'd never seen him so focused. He was *Alf*, sure enough, but a more serious Alf. You could see it in his attitude.

On the Tuesday we decided to have a half-hour fitness check, and Alf got wind of it at breakfast. Uptight, he was, like really uptight. Here was a strong message of his intentions — he was here to show 'em, to show 'em all.

He only ate lightly at breakfast, and at that morning fitness session I'd never seen him put in better. He was up with the leaders in the distance running, and he hates distance running.

Hey guys, he was saying, I'm up to this. It was a powerful message, and a huge message. After that, there were no doubters in the team.

The rest of the week went calmly enough. I stayed in his company a fair bit, and he was just one of the boys down the back of the bus, where he'd always sat. On the day before the game I remember bringing the forwards in, telling them Alf had been part of winning and losing series. "If you blokes don't aim up, he can't do what he wants to do."

Webcke and big Petero, Buttigieg, they aimed up all right.

We know about Game III, about the skill levels, theatrics and heroics. Alf, he'd been targeted for a decade, this little player who can't be targeted. The jinking runs, the kicks . . . I don't remember how many tries he scored for the Broncos, but I'll never forget the one he scored that night for Queensland.

With 20 minutes to go, yes, it was me who started the chant in the stands: "Alfie! Alfie! Alfie! . . ." I thought, I'm going to enjoy this. So I did.

I've seen a few pictures of us in a bear hug afterwards, the look of delight and relief at the fine line we had walked. People still suggest I gambled that night, but they are not people who know me — because I don't gamble.

When Alf left the Broncos that first time I wanted to give him a farewell but couldn't; it just wasn't the time.

Then this. ANZ Stadium has never erupted like it did that night. Alf was back. He never lets anyone down, this absolute champion of our game.

Over time you find faults with lots of people, and athletes, in particular, can find trouble. But while no one with the exception of Peter Jackson has ever had a better time, Allan Langer has never done a thing to bring this game into disrepute.

Tell your kids: have a great time, enjoy your sport like Alf did. And learn that you can have fun without being an idiot.

The Courier-Mail either didn't or couldn't print enough papers the morning after, when every Queenslander wanted to read about the fairytale that came true. At the airport later on there was just him and me, that's all. I thanked him, and I don't think I've ever seen him look so happy. I reckon he could have floated back to England.

Within weeks Alf was back to live in Australia, arriving the week the Broncos were playing Cronulla in Sydney. I asked him down, as you do, and walked into the ground to see him being mobbed by kids. I walked over and said, "Mate, I've made you famous."

He just looked and smiled. Champions don't need to talk.

EPILOGUE

An Australian Story ...

WE JUST HAVE TO DO OUR BEST

EARLY IN OUR PARENTING LIVES WE MADE A DECISION, FULLY aware of the difficulties our children — Justin, Elizabeth and Katherine — had in front of them. We wanted them to be independent and to be themselves.

We have never hidden our kids or been embarrassed by them; it's just that outside our circle we wanted to protect them. And we did. My so-called profile meant that our family would be a "good story" and that sooner or later the media would want to intrude into my life and our lives. And as the kids progressed and grew into adulthood, there was a period when I was approached by a number of commercial stations with offers to do stories on us.

When I say, "I feel we have a story to tell", it's just that there is no manual for raising children, especially children with disabilities. Yet, suddenly, we had two of them.

After Justin and Katherine were born, people would say things like, "God only gives children like these to special people who can handle it." We struggled to handle it. From the very beginning, we knew we weren't special — we just had to do our best to meet the responsibilities we now had.

Australian Story, along with Vanessa Gorman and Phillipa Quinn, approached us in 1999. It was the first time I had taken an offer seriously. I'd watched *Australian Story* a few times and I talked it over with a friend who is in the industry. He said it would probably be the best and most ethical way to tell our story, the way it was and is . . . the way it should be told.

I came home one night and brought the subject up with the girls. I said I was ready to do it, but only if we were all ready to do it. My wife Trish was hesitant, and most times the girls have similar views to Trish, this time Katherine especially.

After our discussion we decided to meet with the ABC. Because of my prickliness with the media, the ABC decided to send two journos who had nothing to do with sport. Our meeting with them pretty much sealed it, mainly because the producer (Vanessa) had no preconceived opinion of who or what I was about. We trusted them not to blow it out of proportion or put a "slant" on it.

As a family we have only watched the show once. I found it very awkward to watch because I really didn't want to relive the experience of talking about ourselves. Trish found it most difficult, as she has never been one to make private things public.

We are constantly taken aback by the response to the show that we received and continue to receive. We never imagined our story would touch so many people in so many different ways. We have received some magnificent letters from parents who, like us, have children with disabilities, and I know the tape is used a lot throughout different organisations, such as schools. The feedback from teachers is quite overwhelming.

My girls are completely over the show, all for their own reasons. Kath's reason, however, amuses me the most. Since the show aired she has lost a lot of weight and now wishes that she had not been frozen in one time in her life. As her father, I told her the real reason is vanity — and she totally agrees.

My mum loved seeing herself on TV. On the show mum is being asked about the knockers and she says, "Those bastards, where are they now?" That response has got a lot of response. Love ya, Mum.

But no one loved it as much as Justin did. We have dubbed a copy for Justin with all the pieces that were cut from the show. When we first showed it to him he watched it for three days straight, calling us all in at different times to watch it with him. He would love to be a pro footballer; actually, he thinks he is. He has really got himself a cult following, and has even been known to sign autographs. Whenever the Broncos or Queensland are playing, he wears the opposition's jersey.

Trish and I often reflect on how lucky we are to have three children whom we love, but more importantly like.

I couldn't have achieved the things I have without Trish. If she hadn't have been so supportive of everything I wanted to do I would not have been able to coach. If you are looking for the success story in this family, then it is Trish, not me. I've never met a person who can continually give so much and require so little back.

People ask what motivates me. My children motivate me. The character they show every day. When I reflect on our children I am proud of them all, proud of what they have achieved. Justin, Elizabeth and Katherine are the children Trish and I were given to care for. You want everything for your children. To you, our lives are different; to us, they are normal. We keep moving on. As parents we didn't treat our children any differently just because they had disabilities; and we didn't ever want them thinking they were different.

Our middle child, Beth, who doesn't get much of a start in this piece, is someone I really respect and admire, not just as a daughter but as a person. I have never heard her wishing things were different. She's had to make sacrifices in a house that revolves around Justin and, at times, Katherine. There were and still are things we couldn't do with her because it would have meant excluding our other two. Something we are not prepared to do.

My two daughters are beautiful, well adjusted individuals. They are best friends. Kath provides something special for Beth, and vice versa. What they share — what we all share — I hope will last forever.